SNORTED THE MOON

AND DOUSED THE SUN

Edited by
Deanne Meeks Brown and Raundi Moore-Kondo

For anyone who has ever been hooked—

For what is a poem but a hazardous attempt at self-understanding: it is the deepest part of autobiography.

                                          – Robert Penn Warren

LETTERS FROM YOUR FEARLESS EDITORS

Dearest reader,

It is difficult to say exactly where this anthology began. Maybe it was when I was a little girl, and I first heard the stories of my father wrestling my drunk grandfather to the ground after chasing my grandmother with a butcher knife through their six bedroom Tudor home only a short walk from where Bill W. and Dr. Bob gathered for the first Alcoholics Anonymous meetings in Akron, Ohio. My grandfather drank tumblers of vodka like water straight from the tap. No ice. As far as my family knows, he never made it to those meetings. He died before I was born.

Or maybe this anthology began on my fourteenth birthday when my mother bought me my first book of poems, *Notes to Myself: My Struggle to Become a Person* by Hugh Prather. I drank up each poem like my grandfather drank vodka, enrolled in a creative writing course at school and wrote my first poem:

> Each night as I lie awake in bed
> I think about tomorrow
> And the things which lie ahead
> For tomorrow is my future
> And I do believe
> It is up to me
> To make it what I see

Or maybe this anthology began the night I told my husband-to-be I would not marry him unless he quit drinking. He quit. We got married. Not fully understanding the complexities of addiction, seventeen years and three children later, I found myself gazing uncomfortably at a sea of anticipatory eyes, as I asked, "Is this not Al-anon?" The man at the podium politely explained that Al-anon was down the hall. This was AA. I had taken a wrong turn. Apologizing, I quickly gathered my belongings and ran for the exit; the only sound coming from my high heels clicking on the tile floor. In an effort to redeem myself, I turned around and confessed, "The way things are going in my life, I may be back here soon." The room exploded with laughter.

Or maybe this anthology was conceived the day my friend and greatest ally, Raundi Moore Kondo, invited me to my first poetry reading. Soon after, we wrote a chapbook, *The Hills are Alive*, and traveled from open-mic to open-mic: Raising awareness, funds, and eyebrows in the fight against breast cancer for which I had been diagnosed a year earlier.

Or maybe this anthology was born the first night I slept in a dorm room on a campus three thousand miles from home—Goddard College—a place Alan Ginsberg once called "The center of the Universe", as I began my pursuit of a Master's in Clinical Counseling and Psychology, took an addictions counseling course, and told my professor, Wendy, "I have an idea." Thus, the book you are now holding in your hands was conceived.

Or maybe this anthology doesn't have just one beginning but has many beginnings; initial stages, first phases, and false starts. Maybe this anthology is my way of making sense of it all, or giving back, or paying it forward or moving forward. Maybe it's not any of the above or maybe it's all of the above. I don't know. It's difficult to say exactly. That is why there is poetry.

Poetry gives voice to the events we don't understand or are too hard to say. Poetry allows us to open doors to the deep labyrinth of our subconscious. Poetry tolerates our ever-changing emotions, moods, and relationships with others and ourselves. Poetry helps us to shape the raw material of our lives into something more comprehensible. Not just into language but also into symbols and code, allowing us to reflect on feelings and events in our lives that are seared on our souls with pain and/or love and/or fragility and/or strength. For when the reality is too painful and exact words too difficult to find or horrendous to speak, writing in metaphor gives us a platform acting as a bridge—spanning and providing passage towards reflection and expression—leading not only to change and healing but to transformation.

Charles Bukowski once wrote, "Writing is the ultimate psychiatrist." And Aristotle discovered that writing poetry allowed people "to transform their problems into power and their sadness into strength" (taken from Furman et al, p. 147). In fact, Vancouver Island University, Jenifer Mullett's 2008 research revealed that articulating one's experience in a creative format such as art, poetry, and song, facilitates healthy changes and growth in a person's life. That is what we hope writing poems for this anthology not only did for the authors of this book but does for the readers as well.

Before you turn the page, we would like to take a moment to thank all of the courageous individuals who submitted their raw, authentic and deeply personal poetry, gave voice to their pain, and delved into their dark side, or humorous side, or bright side and presented their beautiful imperfect selves to us all. Because only in this way, when we dare to share our most honest and vulnerable selves and feel part of something bigger, can we transform our problems and find some semblance of self-love and acceptance. Something we all need as the New York Times recently reported that opiates are now the number one killer of Americans under the age of fifty. We hope you too, dear reader, will find peace within the pages of this book as you enter the world of addiction and redemption through each of these brave and heroic poets.

Love,
Deanne

LETTERS FROM YOUR FEARLESS EDITORS

Dear Word Lovers,

The most important thing I have learned from being a teacher is that words do not teach: Experience teaches. Perhaps that is why teachers give homework, and why I am drawn to poetry. Poetry has the potential to be so much more than mere words. A great poem is a vivid and palpable experience: A hi-def, virtual reality, full-contact sport with Dolby Surround Sound, Smell-O-Vision and possible loss of bodily fluids. A poem can allow one to walk a mile in another's stilettos without breaking an ankle. This collection of poetry is like a stroll through a funhouse full of mirrors. You will undoubtedly catch glimpses of yourself everywhere you look, faces you haven't seen in ages and distorted angles you have never dared to reflect on. Reading these poems may cause a strong case of déjà vu because metaphorically we've all been there before. I believe it is through poetry that we can truly learn from each other and feel a little less alone while doing it.

For the Love of Words,
Raundi

SNORTED THE MOON

AND DOUSED THE SUN

JOHN GARDINER

Junkie Blues

I've been a cold as iceberg junkie, a whoring drunk -- I snorted the moon and doused the sun with gasoline, walked the streets of New York City gripped by monkey claws. I've been down to 34th St. to pick up some ounces of gold rock, got my manitol, my blade, my grinder, got my beer and joints and cigarettes; let's make up some grams and party down -- hey, it's a good count, we got enough blow for a week, we gotta stave off the blues... Tim Hardin's on the radio with his beautiful haunting voice, he overdosed on smack a few weeks after John Lennon died and no one seemed to care. Tim Hardin got a hot shot and reeled himself in -- I better get straight, I gotta audition for a play on 46th St., my nose is running like an open drain, fire-red and burned out like an old stump... All the artists are running to their graves like lemmings over a ledge, the children of the moon can't make it through the day, can't make it back to night before the unsavory sun gives way. I've been down to the bus station at 3 in the morning to stash 10 grand of speed, I'm a cocaine cowpoke, got a bronco under me kicking the life out of my soul, I gotta get out -- I wander freak-eyed through Port Authority followed by goblins, I scare the pimps and hookers, stand out like a transvestite -- I saw Walt Whitman over by the vegetables. I gotta get out, gotta move, gotta pack into the back country and follow John Muir, leave these skyscrapers behind and find some cold mountain streams.

LINDA SINGER

Addiction

My Buddhist monkey mind
climbs trees,
throws coconuts
down, down on me.
Each has a name,
his name,
craved with a knife.
Think,
I will not think
about his marmalade words,
about how they taste
good with tea.
Just one
time more
sweet words.
The stone heart,
I leave fingerprints
in his rock stone heart.
His love a hole in the sand,
falling, crumbling, an avalanche.
My words washing in, filling
up emptiness with seawater,
salty to the tongue.
Sweetness diluted
in hard stone.
Caught in tangled roots,
uprooted roots,
grabbing at air,
gasping at air.
I will not think about him,
think about thinking
about him.
He is not going to call,
I'm not going to call,
I stop,
thinking about him.
Monkey mind stop. Stop.

SARAH THURSDAY

What To Do With Empty Hands

I don't know what to do with my hands
I opened them up, I released my grip
the rope was ripped away
last strands tangled in my fingertips
so I cut one thread at a time
with the razor of my teeth

I still don't know what to do with my hands
I washed off the blood, cleaned out the burn
they are bandaged and gauzed
but my fingers keep curling
around the ghost of your wrists
I press them out flat against the shower wall
against my bedroom wall, one hand
against the other, finger to finger

I still don't know what to do with my hands
I've been writing you out of my heart for months
I run out of lead, I run out of paper
still my hands move around the ghost of your neck
your voice murmuring in the center of my palms
I try but I can't suffocate your shadows

I don't know what to do with my hands
so I press them to my mouth
let my lips surrender to your memory
I drag them everywhere you've been
across the back of my thighs
down the tip of my nose
they circle the round of my shoulder
(the last place you ever kissed me)

GRAHAM SMITH

fuck pumps and perfume
loves to seduce, the first time's
always such a rush

PEGGY CARTER

Seduction

I swore I'd never go down that road again
But here I am like the drunk at the bar, begging
For one more touch, one more kiss, one more drink at your spring.

It was the spring of eternal loving
And I drank deeply
Now, every cell of my body swims in that spring.
And still I thirst

Those were sunny, loving days
I had no idea where I was going
Could it be
I shouldn't have opened that door.

But you held out your hand so tenderly
I had no choice
Your name was power
And your love held so much promise

You gave me dreams, dreams that haunt me still
I wake covered in sweat
My heart craters and breaks
My body shakes
I turn and thrash in the bed, looking for release, for comfort

And there is none.

For I have been seduced
by you

last surge of kimberly yates

you've return again
clawing memory
onto ash latent bones

your voice caught
in webbing limbs
of dead branches

your lingering smile
rustles through
fallen leaves

i taste your scent
alongside the mist
the sweet saccharine
i drank myself
silly on

only now
you are shaped
w/ memory
& tremor

& leaving you
in the nakedness of silence
has me exposed
wallowing in mulch mud

even now
in my smallest hour
w/ dust gnawing my corpse

it is you
who has me
rotting away

BRITTANY THALER

Obsession #2

there's an allure about her that ropes you in.
smooth with her words
coy with her eyes
when she aimed for you, her lasso never missed.

it was her cool demeanor that made you long to know her.
she always ended the night first, always
had other things to do
like read about the world.
shelves lined with books
walls lined with lists she
was a force of something with a script in her hand
forever playing the part
of ringleader in her own circus she
was so filled with charisma
that you rearranged the universe to have dinner with her
(and you didn't realize it until
after you picked up the check).

when her lasso came for me, the throw was a perfect ten:
she was the new drama teacher
I was her technical director
and life
felt like publishers clearing house just wouldn't stop calling.
I was so entranced
that I never even felt
her rope on my skin.
we were The Unstoppable Force
two coasters racing alongside each other
flying fast with no troubles in sight.

but all coasters reach the end of the line
and The Unstoppable Force always meets The Immovable Object.
feelings collided with denial
and the last of the tracks launched me head first

into the sad pile of broken stuff
a place where she abandoned those who got close enough to see
the whites of her eyes.
she
was annie oakley with a rifle
and I had only ever been
the tin can with a bullseye.

getting out
was like trying to climb a wall of dirt
a few steps, then my footing caved
and I fell like I always did
at 4am
on the floor of my bathroom
beaten down by the remains of empty night.
no stars then, no pinprick fire flies to guide me I
drowned in memories that crashed against my sinking ship
another steamer
swallowed by the waves, slipping down through the cold
falling far below the surface
sos, I called out
but my words were met only with silence.

in the aftermath, the days were the same.
the morning started when reality struck
leaving a handprint of her absence reverberating in my head.
next came the nausea as I sat on the cold tile
arms gripping the trash can tightly—
but the sickness was in my mind, and you can't run away from the
thoughts in your head.
withdrawal surrounded me, sewed its feet to mine like peter pan's
shadow
it was everywhere when I tried to distract myself from
loss of appetite
weakness
crying
restlessness
nervousness
trembling
depression

anxiety
insomnia
clammy skin
racing thoughts
loss of interest or pleasure in activities she
was the dopamine released in my brain
and without her, the scales inside me were so off-balance
that lady justice and the strength of the titans weren't enough
to pull me out of myself.

the hardest part of withdrawal
was fitting my life around it.
on my first day as a college technical director it
didn't want to get up
it
wanted to lay in bed
and watch me star in the brand new film called She Can't Handle
This.
by the time morning woke the sun
I was ready for my afternoon nap.

with the help of my remaining pride
I drove to the school
in the cloud of daze that wrapped itself around me.
the 4am routine was draining
but missing it was against the rules.
sleep called out from behind my eyes
but I had more pressing matters
like fighting my feeling
of being squeezed inside a box
by the fears that inched closer and closer, the voices
swarmed round my head, stingers out
angry words injected
panic
anxiety
cry
pass out

shut down
fail

withdrawal
clung to my back as I climbed out of my car
this was my circus now
and the only one in the ring was me.

when I walked inside, anxiety did too
stomping hard on the backs of my shoes
close enough for me to feel it's breath on my neck
so I took a step, and turned the key in the door.
just a few hours of swatting away those thoughts, a few hours of pretending to be
something other than myself.
each thought and word and thing I did
would will the ticking hands of the clock forward.

time chugged on, and I trudged along with it.
I followed every step
in the book called How to Avoid Getting Fired From Your Dream Job.
I was so focused that I didn't notice
how each moment was charging
the battery in my soul, refilling
just enough of me that I started to feel purpose
beyond belonging to someone else I
was my own technical director
and in those moments, I decided that
instead of picking up the check, I'd ask the waiter to split it.

at the end of the day, I turned the key in my door
4 am would still come like a freight train, but work had busied my nerves just long enough
to crack a window on the box that trapped me
letting some of my fears squeeze out into the july night.
I turned to withdrawal and remarked
one full day at the circus with no casualties.
it sneered and rolled its eyes
but the next morning, when I tried to loosen its straps
it finally let me.

LYNNE BRONSTEIN

Free

Set me free, she said.
I can no longer be
Your harem girl.

I see you in my dreams
when I never expect to.
Our time was long ago.
Our love is nothing.
I lift my hands to you
Cuffed but holding the key.
Unlock me and end
This enjoyable misery.

Free from what
He said.
I never told you what to be.
You brought me drinks.
You gave me candy.
You followed me for miles
Along the roads of LA summer.
You wanted this
As you wanted me.
I never led the way.
There are no ropes or chains
Around your wrists.
We've said our goodbyes
And we are friends
eternally.
I hold no key.
But I'm haunted
She cries.
Why do you stay within me?
Night after night
And during afternoon naps
You come to me.

Sometimes we kiss.
Sometimes you judge me harshly.
Once I dreamed of you
Lying upon a surgical table.
You begged me not to operate.
You were the helpless one!
I could have taken the knife
And ended this.

I know I could make you
Go away.
I could close my eyes,
Blow you out
And make a wish
To bring to me
A harmless love
That will leave no trace.

She knows that she is free.
She carries the men she has loved
Like beautiful bugs caught in amber
And she doesn't give them up
Because she likes too much
The fun of handling
And ogling them.
She knows
That what they have given of themselves
She owns forever,
That what she gave them is theirs,
Yet she never loses
What is rightly hers.

There's no human connection
without imagination's chain
and there's no guilt
and no one to blame.

CINDY RINNE

Attachment to Belonging

Attachment to Belonging

For years I think loyalty is my addiction. A steadfast allegiance.
Unswerving.

Attachment to Identity

> *I am a master builder. Sometimes when I build, my little*
> *Brother eats a Lego. I tell him 'no' and he starts to cry.*
> The Five-year-old

Understanding opens as I realize attachment is my addiction.
The tape of needing praise and to be the most important is on redial.
He asks, Where is Cindy? We can't pray without her. If my position
At church is threatened, envy sets in like a mother lion protects
Her cubs. I despise and discount the healer or the singer who seem
To try to take my place. I am a dandelion growing through the crack
In the driveway.

Attachment to Importance

> *The run was icy. The daughter slid and fell onto her mother.*
> *They skidded down the mountain. They were lucky not to get hurt.*
> The Stranger

After I left this situation, where I gave much of my time fastened to him
Like a band aid, he never asks me to coffee. I reach for breath like a lotus.
He has dinner with the friends I lose because I was faithful to his opinions
On how a church should be run.

Attachment to Praise

> *I have a friend who believes she has one wing Quaker and one wing*
> *Buddhist, but I have many wings.*
> The Visitor

Over and over I hear from my friend, You are the best. You get me.
One day. One sentence. This ends like a cactus stings. I hear rejection,
Not good enough, and I was thrown into a deep pit.

Attachment to Excellence

Move forward as the way opens.
The Mystic

This time the journey leads me back. A new style appears. New fabrics
And threads. I stitch crocheted doilies, vintage handkerchiefs, and cotton
Fabrics of children chasing fireflies.

Going forward means learning to trust again without the need to possess,
Cling to, and control. My value like young basil grows.

TRISTA HURLEY-WAXALI

Spring Vegetable Lamb Stew

I knew we evolved into a problem when I typed in the search bar "L" for lamb stew recipes and got lawyers. Not just ones from around here but also in Silicon Valley, each asking to do an initial call to see if 'we were right for each other.' I wasn't looking for an intimate conversation but whether or not peas cooked well with asparagus. I checked the bank account and thought we deserved to splurge tonight as the cheque cleared for Mr. Intimate who guaranteed us we were represented. He mentioned that a better pairing will be turnips near the end of our first call. Maybe I made the mistake of answering while browsing, either way, I remember how helpful he was like a valet driver to getting on Melrose Ave. For this was my inability to draw healthy boundaries that needed to be re-surveyed. To stop digesting the constraints of day-to-day updates within the company.

I needed to let go of the rush to success. My heart tightening from the anticipation of hearing the words 'closed the round' or 'new hire,' to photo's of random people encouraging the brand popping up on social media. To reading articles mentioning the funds raised and technological advancements, we stood out like a centerfold. And then one day, he hit rock bottom. He realized there was no longer a lump sum but rather he was gambling with his present opportunities for a future payout that might not exist. Maybe that possibility was there before the greed kicked in from the investors. Or maybe this is how to operate, expecting you to ride out the false high over the next number of weeks. I couldn't do it anymore, whatever the company was doing I was no longer interested. I needed us to find our love again for food.

The apartment held the thick scent, dishes piled in the sink and the garbage infused with stems. Rosemary, thyme and sage, reflecting the advice I was ready to dish out by the bowls. He opened the door and the smell slapped him in the face. I begged him to come back to the home, to stop what he's doing in this pursuit. To created the boundary with our love again. We should stop chasing the titles that come with the culture of reinventing and embrace who we are. He an inventor and I the writer- not the CTO or the interim assistant. He saw in this moment how I was past caring about his daily stand ups and any insight into leads. Or it will be what leads us apart. That we need to better focus the power, to no longer chase the payout. So now we seek the power that flows throughout our home, that keeps the oven on: at a steady 350 degrees.

BECCA GAFFRON

Struggling To Achieve Some Edgy
Four Minute Climax

It all came down to mortality. Mostly his. These days, every cigarette felt like a "fuck you" to middle-age and whatever the hell came after it. "We can't choose who we fall in love with," he told her—that woman who loved him hard, even now. And he loved her back. But theirs wasn't a hurtling down the highway at 110mph, drunk and whooping at a moonless sky, kind of love. It didn't make him feel ten feet tall and bulletproof.

His eyes dodged hers as he spoke, ashamed by his choice to disregard their quiet affection for the sake of someone new. But there was plenty of life left in this ol'boy and he just needed a little flash bang to prove it. He wanted to swan dive off the gossamer wings of his new-found twenty-something, all-about-me girl. To taste the whiskey-like heat of conquest and ego when his thrusting desire pierced the veneer of her perpetual resting-bitch face.

In those moments, he could convince himself it was love. He pretended the way she fed on him, greedily consuming all his assets, was the purest form of affection. He stopped eating, as if to prove he needed the nothing she offered. He focused on her rare trickles of vulnerability as they leaked onto his calloused fingers, and played them back to her gently, believing it was their song. And for a few blissed-out moments, he forgot his graying beard and thinning hair. Forgot his fear that the best adventures had already come and gone. Forgot that life is complicated.

So his eyes dodged from that woman who loved him heart and hands, with a kind of love that's willing to put in the work. He turned away, called another darling. He would be her daddy and her lover, lost in a twisted fiction of simplicity and young again. Struggling to achieve some edgy four-minute climax—one for every decade he'd used up—before she sucked him dry and moved on, leaving only a faint fetid scent and the lingering memory of young skin.

BECCA GAFFRON

Instagram Poem #34

Drums pound in the deep, but all you get's reverberation. You, a hero in sheep's clothing. Anger is your wolf. Hit first, hit hard. That will make things right. Then put on your suit-coat of obligation, snazzy enough for the hum-drum muzak you live to now. Happy is for pussy-men. Ignore the dirty rhythms that speak to your soul. Ignore art. Except the little bits needled on your skin. Pain is a sensation and suffering is where it's at. What real men do. Smash things to the beat, maybe you will feel. Something. Anything. In this sleep of video games and broken dreams you've chosen, what hope may come? 'Cause numb is not the same as alive. And you are far from comfortable. Or comforting. You get by holding tiny hands. Daddy is the man. But she doesn't make you strong, you know? I'll tell you a secret, she's the strong one. Sensitivity, compassion, doubt, second chances? There is no place in your man's world for that kinda strength. No quarter for the shit you fear. Yet you are frayed. You've come undone, once or twice in the echoing alone of your perfect home. Shhh...it's our secret. So lose yourself in those easy subtle addictions--other women, juniper fumes, and greed. And by the way, what is your fair share of something someone else worked for? We all know, it's as much as you can take. Grab it with both hands. Avoid the ugly truth staring back at you from the bathroom mirror-- you have everything you (n)ever wanted.

Previously appeared in *Camroc Press Review & Honest Lies and Imaginary Truths*

After the 2016 Election (and/or)
A Whiskey Shot for Your Thoughts, My Beloved

We buy each other liquid love offerings.
One bottle of Tito's vodka
in his left hand and in my right hand
organic Chardonnay
with dinner, with baseball,
it's kind of a condiment
in lieu of compliments.

Our right hands pledge allegiance
to alcohol's healing properties,
to keep our romance lubricated,
to toast our waning fortune,
to scoff at death together
with a shot of oaky distillery
amber fireballs, whiskey

for our whiskers, counteract
this misery aging us.
Our roster of dysfunctions
drown in souvenir mai-tai glasses,
Insecurities to the attic, we gonna dance-
stumble, saunter, prance
tourists in a few sips of bitter nectar

a greyhound for my imaginary pet,
a Cape Cod for all the places
we will never visit, why go?
Airlines are stingy on libations.
We go cheap, but fast to visit
reruns of Cheers, find bars nearby
Lusciously we can rest assured

Meanwhile, we pickle internal organs
we'll be able to teleport not far off,

technology will save us from our idiocracy or
beam us to a dive bar now decades closed.
We'll linger there on the precipice
a tilted downhill dance floor littered with empty bottles
our glazed days before us invisible, inevitable ice
clattering glass we phantoms fragment ourselves
behind dusty blinds
watching mayhem masquerade
as matrimony. Go on suckers, go ahead and bite that worm.
Contentment can be substituted for a small container,
a small price of admission, what's a liver
transplant between old friends?

DEANNE MEEKS BROWN

Dear Sugar Daddy

Oh Henry, it was not because of *Clark*
You would have killed me before long if I continued to indulge in
your divine sweetness.
Like oxygen is to fire
You stoked my sweet tooth
And fed my cancer
How I craved you

Your milk chocolate *Kisses*
And *Gummi Bear* hugs
Melted me
And that almond nougat center of yours
Stuck to my insides
Your *Laffy Taffy* tongue could undo me in one licking
And the way you commanded those black licorice whips
You brought me to my knees
I prayed for salvation
As you placed *Necco Wafers* in my palm
Body of Christ
Amen

I still remember the day we met
I hit *Payday*
You were pure *Almond Joy*
With your strawberry Starburst smile
And *Milky Way* eyes
I was on *Cloud 9*
You always had that effect on me

Like the day we played double dare with X rated candy hearts
You wrapped me in *Bubble Gum Tape*
Tootsie rolled me in your *Pop Rocks* quarry
And fun dipped me in your old fashioned soda fountain
I was a red hot *Atomic Fireball*
Boom

Or the time we arm wrestled for first *Dibs* on that blue raspberry
flavored *Blow Pop*
You won
The bubble popped
The gum stuck in my hair
We tried to wash it out with peanut butter cups
But it was of no use
I had to cut it all off
Every last strand
I knew then that I was in love

Then there was that infamous night you gave me a candy
diamond ring
Down on one knee
You asked me to marry you
I slowly sucked the precious stone down to the stump
My saliva dissolving the red jewel down to a syrupy puddle
in my heart
And said "yes"

You were my *Sugar Daddy*
And I wanted to have your *Sugar Babies*

Damn, how I loved to climb your *Mountain Dew* six pack
Count how many licks it took to get to your *Tootsie Roll* center
Tickle your *Skittles*
Wiggle your *Joe Joe's*
Butterfinger your doughnut hole
And get lost in your package of *Whoppers*
Drunk on your liquid cherry cordial insides
I would howl at the *Peppermint Patty* Moon
While I prayed to the sugar gods for more

But like all good things, it had to come to an end
I could not live on sugar alone
My doctor said no more
To keep my cancer from coming back
We were both devastated
After being joined at the hip, like melted Junior Mints

But instead of ending things, I became bitter trying to change you
I stripped you from your bright colors, sugar coating, and gooey caramel filling
Took away your nuts, your sprinkles, and your *Good Humor* candy center crunch
But as I tried to soften your insides it only hardened your shell
And we ended up in *Big Hunk* fights

When I finally realized changing you would not work
I tried to quit cold turkey, complete abstinence
I cleaned out my cupboards
Threw out my hidden stash
And poured every ounce of you down the drain
But I became delirious
And my hallucinations got the best of me
Gummi Worms were crawling all over my skin
And *Swedish Fish* were swimming in my eyeballs

So lastly, I attempted to replace you with other sweeteners
But there was no substitute for you

I was in such denial baby
Quitting you was like trying to bite through a jawbreaker
You were my crack
My dopamine *Ding Dong*
Bursts of euphoria would rocket me straight to Mars when you entered my bloodstream
No amount of *Good and Plenty* could satisfy me
And my willpower was no match to your *Pixie Stick*
How I wanted to pour every last sugary granule down my throat
Let you dissolve in my mouth
Enter my veins
And travel to every corner of my being

Until one day, I hit rock candy bottom
I could not bear to live without you
So I drank an entire case of *Coca-Cola*
Swallowed the *Bottle Caps* too
And hung myself from the rafters with *Red Cherry Twists*
They untwisted

I fell to the ground
Smashing into a thousand little *Reese's Pieces*

That was when I finally admitted I was powerless over you
And came to believe that a power greater than me could restore
my sanity
I began to let go
Joined Sweet Things Anonymous
Went to my meetings
Found a *Mentos*
Read my literature
And worked my twelve step program
They were my *Lifesaver*

Since my spiritual awakening, I live a healthier life style
Green juice and flax seed cookies have replaced those late night
candy bars, butterscotches, and lemon drops

But I still long for you
Dreaming of those sweet lazy daze tangled in each other's arms
Giggling at the comic strips wrapped around little pink *Bazooka*
rectangles
Melted, hot, and sticky in a pile of wrappers and empty bottles of
root beer
Puffing on bubble gum cigarettes
While the room filled with powdered sugar smoke

DERRICK ORTEGA

Habits (formerly known as Jigsaw Limbs)

Saccharin rides the fractures of my snakeskin boots. Through an angled mirror, I imagine a crystalline swarm—white blood cells prowling on a diabetic silhouette. It's okay: my shadow is an addict. So is the hand that granulates, pouring into a footprint of black snow.

This Time

It will be perfect, yes it will –
this time

The sun and the wind played with the clouds while
the room where we
lay
flashed with sunlight and darklight...

This time it will be perfect he
said as he touched my face
and then my
breast
and the smile in his eyes echoed mine.

The sun and the wind played outside our room
and the skies spoke our names...

As we spoke
our love...

That union was ours and yes it was
perfect, as perfect as he'd said it would be.
In a thousand years there will never be
another love like his was
for
me.

The sun and the wind played with the clouds as we lay
in each others arms.
From that love came the longing for more...

And always and always it will be –

perfect.

This time.

BECCA GAFFRON

The Bad Boys

Addicts:
Do you know the maudlin man,
the maudlin man,
the maudlin man?
Do you know the maudlin man,
who lives on dreary lane?

Survivors:
Sheer will drives heart beats
beats giving up or in
in a perpetual state of loss.

Demons:
Embrace your demons,
if they're the only ones
who bothered to stick it out for the long haul.
But even as their sturdy arms
cradle your broken self,
remember they take another piece each time.

And they will never make you whole.

CLIFTON SNIDER

True Love

My GPS guides me through
unknown territory,
undeveloped landscape of rugged
Southern California hills,
San Gabriel Valley,
clotted with townhouses
packed tight,
and I hear a Cole Porter song
on my iPod,
"True Love,"
sung by Elton John & Kiki Dee.

Why does his image
penetrate my mind?

Some layer of my nervous system,
some portion of my brain,
some muscle
--call it my heart--
belongs to him.

He was my "happy place"
when the dentist drilled
or the surgeon cut,
when we looked to each other,

by turns embraced on the bed,
and I ignored the stench of liquor
on his breath, malady
that poisoned our togetherness,
twisted and strangled
his brain cells,
sullied but did not kill
my heart,
my stubborn heart.

SARAH THURSDAY

Your Dark Sunlight

You, carried by wind, fill my horizon
I am tangled in your kite strings
knees bloody from the drag
arms ache from wind yanking

I squeeze eyelids tight
can't find sleep in your sunlight
eyes grow dark
circled by your high maybes

Your wild flight, soar and dive
I have no wings to carry
can't pull to your height
you only rise, grow farther

Hand me your knife
cut me clean of you
Let my wrists bleed and clot
let me fall asleep

in the quiet dark

The Hunter Ring

sawdust on their tack

swims in the air,

-brushed by dust-covered horsetail-

Falls to the ground to

join feathers of peacocks

on spilt Ace compound that

Fell from the corner of a sad pony's

mouth, who just looks sleepy now-

like every good pony should

when a child is on his back.

CHRISSIE MORRIS BRADY

Need

He once said
he was addicted to early recovery.
The pain in that
overwhelms me.

Some would call
him a dickhead, timewaster,
Some habits
are hard to break.

He once swallowed
the ounces of cocaine
he just bought
when cops pulled up.

A week in jail,
suspended sentence.
Suspicious of all,
we lost touch.

I face my codependence,
the need to fix him.
It's hard since he fits
the holes in my soul.

CHRISTINE ISHERWOOD

Cold, hard beds

Adorned in your fury, dressed in your rage,
if I do not recognize myself in the mirror,
there's no one to blame.
Shards scattered in mayhem, I gathered up,
and wove of them my magnificent hide.
Dressed in that discarded,
I shimmer and gleam,
wearing bits of you,
knowing eventually I will disappear
into you.
If I dart into shadows, and linger there too long,
maybe the shadows will eat me up,
maybe they'll become home.

I'm part composed of stories born,
of buried pasts,
of thunderstorms,
of aching hearts,
of cloudy days
and clouded eyes.

I weep in silent graveyards,
lay myself on cold, hard beds,
feel their ache in my bones.
Tears once shed hardened long ago,
and now may only be chipped away as I drape myself in silks
and rags,
and no one may know my name.
I'm the aching part of you,
I'm the hunter, I'm the game.
I try, and I try, and I try.
But oh, the relief of the day,
when the darkness is past.

In the palm of god, he laughs and cackles
as I dive down into the deep blue,

knowing there's no route home;
it has been erased by waters which rise,
and continue to rise.
Time too has eradicated all I once knew and was,
and there is nowhere to go, only to press ever on,
although bridges have been smashed,
brambles guard their secrets,
and the way is arduous.

Through drunken meanderings,
past crazed crossroads,
intermittent highways
and silent paths of gloom,
ever the dark night crosses my soul.

A slip of the lips sent me tripping
through dark forests
wearing the ghosts of lovers past
and calling their names.
Their names find me and bind me,
they do not let me forget,
nor let me rest as their echoes craw and draw in close.
Even though I am alone,
I am surrounded by them,
and they do not release me.
If there were a path I could walk,
I would walk.
If there were a route across the top of the mountains
I would take it.

CLAUDIA DURAN

Mi Querida

Aburrida	Bored
Estoy	I am
Sin Ti En Mi Vida	Without You in my Life
Sin tus fuegos en mi Garganta	Without Your Flames in My Throat
Solita	Lonely
Sin un Trago	Without a drink
De tu sabor	Of Your Taste
En mi boca	In My Mouth
Como te extrano	How I miss You
Cada Noche	Every Night
Contando las horas	Counting down the Hours
Quando te puedo amar	When I can make Love to You
Otra Vez	Once again
Por Favor	Please
Otra !	Again!
Otra!	Again!
Mi Querida - Tequila.	My Dearest – Tequila.
Otra Vez Juntas	Once Again when we're Together
Me haces sentir	You make me feel
Sentimientos Que	Sentiments that
Ni Hombre…	No Man…
Ni MUJER.	No Woman.
Ni nadien Humano	No Human Being
Me forca sentir	Forces me to Feel
Siempre una Dama	You're Always a Lady
Haciendo el Amor	Making Love
Con otra botella	With another Bottle
Adentro de Mi – Cama	Inside of my - bed
Toda la noche	All night long

Mi Haces	You make me
Cantar a la luna	Sing to the Moon
Besando las estrellas	Kissing the stars
Llorando al sol	Crying to the sun
De Cada Manana	of Every Morning
Otra,	Again!
Otra Vez!	Once Again!
Por Favor	Please
Como me puedes	How could you
Dejar a si	Leave me like this
Sin ti	Without you
Sin tu carino	Without your love
Sin tu calor	Without your heat
Por Que Mi Haces Sentir	Why do you make me feel
Un dolor	Such Pain
En mi cuerpo	In my body
Tan miserable	So miserable
En mi Corazon	In my heart
Me das dolor…	You give me a pain…
De la cabeza!	A Headache!
Como me puedes	How could you
Dejar tan cruda!	Leave me so hung over!
Eres maldita	You're a mean one
Traviesa	A troublemaker
Traicionera	A backstabber
Al fin	In the end
Tu gusanito	You're little worm
Mi marea	Makes me dizzy
Enborachandome	Make me drunk
Lagrimas Nublandome	Tears cloud my
Los Ojos	Eyes
Perooo,	Buuuttt,
Con un solo Tragito…	With one little sip…
Me haces Sentir	You make me feel
Galan	Brave

Fuerte
Como Una Reina
Sabrosa
Como tu Sabor de Sal
Jalapeño y Llelo

Te lo juro te quiero
– margarita mia!

Es Verdad que Aburrida
Sin Ti Estoy
Sin Tus fuegos
En mi Vida

Mi Querida…
Tequila.

Strong
Like a Queen
Delicious
Like your taste of salt
Jalapeño and ice

I swear to you I love you
– Margarita of mine!

It's true that I'm bored
Without you
Without your flames
In my life

My dearest…
Tequila.

ELIZABETH ISELA SZEKERESH

This Could Be Me

This could be me
One sip away
Siren call of oblivion
All the times I drove
The Devil in the passenger seat
Me behind the wheel
Of a death machine
The thrill of Sprite
And 90 proof Peach schnapps
In a Del Taco cup
Eighteen
The open road whizzing by
The syrup sweet burn of courage down my throat
Transgression
Nice middle class girl
My friend's fake id
The first puke
I belong
The voices stop
The yets to come
No, your honor
Vertical bars
And prison suits
The brick wall with my name
The fall down the stairs
The gun solution I somehow fuck up
My people live life long
I would not go quick
But suffer many years
And take a few with me
The wavy lines
One eye cocked
To see the road
Reckless thrill of freedom
Disguising

My bondage
My dependent need
Twenty-eight
Fuck it all
Dignity and Self respect
Ghosts
Long ago drunk away
All my money poured down my throat
Dodging traffic stops
Up residential side streets
To make it to my bed five miles away
The last puke
The Devil in the mirror at 3 am
Is Me
She still calls
Years later
When I least expect
The pop of the can
The whiff of wine
Pineapple juice I still can't drink
It wakes up the Bottle Monster
I lick the air for a memory
With my devil's forked tongue
My cells ache and beg
The nuclei cry out
For the liquid misery that soothes me
Coconut rum
Lemon drops
Jack and Diet Coke
At the end, Whiskey shots from the well
No top shelf liquor for me
Dive Bars without windows
Dank with cheap liquor crushed with broken souls
Vacuuming The Lost in
Parking lot cracked by vomit, piss and shredded dreams
A seductive song of promised Relief
Lassos out to drag me
To my false
Home

A deceitful croon
A keening cry
Drink me

Drink me

Drunk me

JERRY GARCIA

Insulation

Oh baby, you were
so out of control,
falling out of your
dance dress
under a narcotic
summer moon.

You thought
you still had it together.

You screeched red terror.
I thought your heart
would tear open right there.
So loudly you roared
"I don't care"
and at that point I saw
the switch to your wits
shut down its current.

That's right—
you didn't care.
You didn't worry about
the confusion of uppers
or downers.

You didn't lose sleep over
thoughts of dehydration,
impending starvation.
So quickly,
like a sponge out of water
your In Style body
became dried flesh.

Now you sprawl on cigarette butts
and dried chewing gum

stiletto heels
awkwardly sidestep
your skeletal frame.

Counting days backwards
your lights dim,
your eyes become two hollow storerooms
insulation as thick
as the buildings around you.
Electrical conductors inert,
spark incomplete,
flashing recall:

champagne flutes
pills by the handful
cocaine lines jump-cutting
to crack pipes

and the sad faces
of former friends—
caretakers held hostage too long
by your ruin.

Repeat

Wrap your lips around me
Inhale me deep
Feel me enter your lungs
Your blood stream
Your heart
Hold
Relax
Breathe out
Long
Steady
Into the air
Flick

Wrap your lips around me
Inhale me deep
Feel me enter your lungs
Your blood stream
Your heart
Hold
Relax
Breathe out
Long
Steady
Into the air
Flick
Repeat
Flick
Repeat
Flick
Repeat

Till you have sucked every last bit of me
Down to the final ash
Till there is nothing left to savor
Nothing left to appreciate

Nothing left
Toss me away
Stomp out my fire
Drag me across the concrete with your rubber sole

Still craving more
You bum another
Repeat

DERRICK ORTEGA

Our Secret Graveyard

Pin your lips on a lit cigarette—
let's look past the horizon
where we will lay, about faced
from the center of this one
last drag, its ash sailing
along the hills of wind wishing
to be a spine. The flesh is empathy.
The dermal, empty. Shove the flux
since dystrophy hungers; its cave moans
with duvet of fog, ill lit and belated
by a minute before, lets sing noir
to the faceless bunch.

GRAHAM SMITH

tried my father's pipe
but those golden leaves i smoked
soon were smoking me

RICHARD NESTER

Hooked

Everything organic is hooked on something,
if only sunlight—the plant's asphalt-busting arrow,
seeds wrapped in time like a syrup, outside will.
Everyone's at the starving end of something,
begging for one more sip—love, danger,
a just-so neatness, the hoarder's fortress of trash.
Art without obsession is a waste, describing humans
without mentioning addiction is impossible.

But none of that is what we mean by hooked,
the choice that chooses you, ever after, the tag
that means you're it. Thirty years ago I quit smoking,
and for twenty years at least had dreams so vivid
I'd wake and not believe I'd really quit. So I know
that quitting can be done, but I also know sometimes
it can't. Jenny Diski, favorite writer of memoirs, dead
of lung cancer, which is why I've never felt heroic—
just lucky, and the most important reason I never
light up now. I might never get that lucky again.

Hooked, hooked up, horny for tomorrow.
Buddha's take it or leave it disinterest ain't
my style, jokester that I am, in the court
of the next and the next after that. "You have
to serve somebody," Dylan said, his skinny
declaration of love: " I never asked much/
I never asked for your crutch/ now don't ask
for mine." If you need it, heed it, sure.
But be the chooser, not the chosen.

I had my reasons for quitting collected
a full year before I stopped. They were too
much like my reasons for continuing—theories.
The worst thing you can have in life is a theory,

a tape that runs over and over till you stop
noticing the new and different. That's another thing
addiction is—a theory, an explanation, a bill of goods
you bought when your resistance was low—
not the key but the lock. Justifying ain't quitting.

Frederick Douglass "there stood slavery . . ."
(Narrative of the Life of Frederick Douglass,
An American Slave, Written by Himself)
freedom far away and slavery familiar,
however terrible,
the best description of bondage I've read
though he wasn't talking about chemicals;
telling us why it was so hard to bust loose
and why even after years of freedom
he "felt [himself] a slave."

The leap is always physical even when
it's spiritual, a two-fisted patience. He had
to beat his overseer half to death, and you
will too—the master in your skin.

There's one more thing I want you to know—
how much I loved it, the family rituals and the
comradeship of fellow smokers. Loved it as
drinkers will, not drunks (abased, degraded),
but drinkers in love with liquor's great romance.
I can't number for you the problems cigarettes
solved—packs a day of problems. Even now,
when I see a cigarette being smoked in a movie,
I feel a sense of communion. To leave that was loss—
the hardest thing—to be exiled, self-banished.
Homer's sirens were but a book-story compared
with that. It was entwined in my nerves.

Tell me what you want to be free of, and I will tell
you how—all I know, which is almost nothing:
bite hard on the hook of something you love
that loves you back and doesn't lie.

JENNIFER BRADPIECE

Sometimes

Our shared lips
and your petal fingers
sometimes pale
to the comfort I kept
in my palm.
The death I breathe
to unpoison myself
and allow
the world to enter
on my terms.
The kindest light
is powder soft.
It burns through my senses-
an execution's charred remains.
Counting away nightmares,
division with a razor blade.
Sniffing the thorns of roses,
their redness bubbles
down my chin,
stains kisses on the mirror-
the window where
I see myself
whenever I look in.
All the lights
thrown on at once
for one brief
brilliant season.

Before it buries me,
I must escape
this toxic Eden.
Although,
at the time
it feels as innocent
as dancing in the snow

as a little girl
at grandpa's house
two days before
Christmas.

BORIS SALVADOR INGLES

to the younger me

wish you were here
sitting on this foldout
holding yesterday's map
across stretched arms

all the junk going in
all the junk going out
like the old days
    remember

all those years ago
scoring nickel bags
in the one ways
in hallways
in alleyways

you died
every night
crucified on patina
burning in soft verdigris

you were
demigod
messiah
false idol

now
you are nowhere
but in
my karma veins

SARAH THURSDAY

Somatic

I can't treat you like phobia
try to desensitize you out of my skin
so that my muscle fibers
won't gather together
at the soft crease of your eyes

      you are not a fear to face
    at the height of a bridge
open my eyes and gaze
    at the depth of you
      lean forward and

                 release

I cannot see you spider
     across my arm
        and deep breathe
    out the shiver
you raise in me

you are less like fear
more like heroin
a need I must starve
from myself
fast out the hunger
until the follicles
in my hair
have escaped
your scent

beautiful junkie

walking back inside
the smell of damped wood
stale coffee
linger throughout
the old room

up on the wall
proverbs read
like scriptures

one step at a time
easy does it
let go   let god

i can still see you
bobbing slowly inside
the crooks of your arms

dark hair
trickling the right side
of your gaunt face

cherry freckles
sitting high
on cheekbones

smile
elongated
& coy

the old timers
called you
   newcomer
pink
dry

just
under
30

but
to me
you were
simply
heroin
chick

D.B.

Heroin Can't Make You a Heroine

It all started with weed,
Then perc 5's and 10's
I wish I was smart enough then
To make amends
Then came the strips and smoking with foil
Boy that's not something you should play with or toil
After 30's and D8's was bath salts
Oh god did I really start to show the world my faults
But just like Newton said
What comes up must go down
I'm lucky I'm not dead
With heroin by my side
I was never alone
Even though I was raised full of pride
You would have NEVER known
I can't remember one time
It went up my nose
Straight to the vein
Is how this story goes
A week then two
Before I knew it Hayleigh wasn't 2
My home was gone
Kids cars and man too
Wake up sick sweating at dawn
You beg you borrow and steal
Just one ticket, will make you able to deal
Where are the girls,
Wow, look how much they grew
This has to stop, it starts with you…
One month clean, then you relapse
Because the world is mean
Oh look a reason, one more trigger
Your mind can't take it
Your emotions take a digger
One day then two days, keep going you'll make it

Remember don't fake it
Before you know
It was worth it to try
One day at a time
Before you know it, you'll be in your prime.

T.W.

Heroin

I was in love with these two things
That took me far away from all things
In reality I used to love them so much
Just to make my body fully numb and my mind fade away
Then I had to run away
I had to let them go
Then I finally got myself together
But I was lost once again
Got involved with a different kind of devil
But on a whole different level
Never knew I could get lost in something so cold as ice
I melted away and it froze me more than twice
I crossed the line too many times before
Running and running for the open door
Praying for the lord to save me only once more.

Save Me

Gripping my veins
He holds me so tight
It's the devils work
He puts up a hell of a fight
I try to let go
But he pulls me back in
Mix up and tie off
Then inject your sin
Every time I'm alone
He's always here
Numbing my pain
And pushing away my fears
You make me forget
All the horrible things
I thought you were perfect
Everything I'll ever need
But as time goes by
My addiction grows stronger
Controlling my life
I can't take it no longer
I'm falling so fast
Harder and harder
Someone please help me
The devil is stronger
Crying so loud
But no one hears a sound
Someone please help me
But I'm never found
And then I woke up
Finally opened my eyes...
I am stronger than this
So from the bottom
I start my fight
Climbing up these walls
With my future in sight

Facing my fears
I put that needle down
This dope will no longer own me
I can turn this all around
In the battle of good and evil
The good always win

Then ready to start the rest of my life
God please wash away my sins.

DAN BURKHARDT

The Insider

As I sit and think things through
I consider how tightly I'll crank down the screw
On the vise that holds my heart and my soul
Can I get those things back?
Will I ever be whole?
I've tried quite effectively to ruin my life
Alcohol, drugs, sex - basic strife
So often I wonder why I'm even here
Why have I been given this life so dear
You know, I've asked, I've prayed really hard
But God, he's quiet, not even a card
For the longest time I was sure God was fake
Well, I've got to tell you, that was a mistake
Looking inside was all it took
And all it took was one good look
He was there all along
Just waiting for me to stop and be strong
It was then that I knew
That my heart and my soul could again be true
I stopped searching outside
For what was inside all along.

Addictions

There are good addictions, a few bad ones too,
Some make us happy, and others make us blue.
Stay with the good ones that give a happy face,
And shun those baddies that lead you to disgrace.
My first addiction is to the GOD that lives,
I could not exist without that which HE gives.
The source of the universe and all within,
HE brought it all forth and caused it to begin.
I'm addicted to the Earth HE gave to us,
She gladly cares for us all and makes no fuss.
I love the mountains and water of the seas,
The green of the grass and the beautiful trees.
Along came family HE gave to each one,
A mother, a daughter, a father and son.
The first social unit, together we cling,
We love them all above every other thing.
Be born in America? I couldn't wait.
They showed me a picture and I took the bait.
Love at first sight, I was addicted for sure,
And still to this day, not looking for a cure.
Addicted to poems, I've written one or two.
When the need for one comes I write it on cue.
I must have been born with a long list in mind
And seem to find one that's just the right kind.
Addictions, they come in all colors and shapes,
And some are hidden behind windows and drapes.
We all have addictions, you can plainly see,
And if they're not so bad, we should let them be.
But if you have addictions that treat you bad
Do not just lay there and wallow in your sad.
Get up and smile, or maybe sing a fun song,
And you'll find something better that makes you strong.

JOSH JENNINGS WOOD

Heaven & Hell

Why shouldn't this be heaven? I remember
hell: coming to in the fake shit apartment
real strangers circled around the table
under the sick dead swing of the ceiling

  fan grasp gaspdizzydizzy slipslipslip

Maybe that wasn't the bottom. Maybe
that stays black and disremembered to push you out

So why shouldn't this be heaven?
Arm invisible
      thrust into the pantry
for carrots or peas or macaroni and cheese
while my baby son dances and my wife laughs
dangerous unfinished still
but ascending ok—
time to adjust to the new view, the rarer oxygen
clumsy unquick climb like up a mountain of spears

TERRY MCCARTY

Fearbasing

Stay home one day, maybe two
No need to go outside

Just wait until provisions are low
Then leave at dusk
Dinner for one
Find a nearly deserted supermarket

Go home and fill refrigerator
Stay up as late as possible
Keep awake until near sunrise
Then try for a restful sleep

As long as you don't dream about
People you could never stop hurting

JENNIFER BRADPIECE

In Praise of Funny Socks

Nobody ever dies in funny socks.
Sure, a clown somewhere,
clobbered by a giant rubber daisy
came to his end
in red floppy oversized shoes.

Funny socks are a safety measure,
I told myself,
on amphetamine-amped nights
alone in the dark,
hugging pillow to chest,
heart pounding through the bedsprings.

Perhaps tomorrow
the last-breath tango
in sparkling stilettos,
lips red and moist as a fresh wound.
But not a solo trembling footnote-death.
So I'd stretch icy feet into the
funniest socks I could find.

Still, some nights,
walking alone on city streets,
perceiving sinister footsteps behind me
my heart pounding into purse straps,
I imagine my feet striding in
fuzzy rainbow toe-sock-steps
and somehow feel safe.

First published in *Media Cakes*

BETSY MARS

Perdition

Seeking solace in ice cream, cream cake,
calorie counting, maintaining a semblance of control,
pounds falling off like ill-fitting jeans.
The anorexic spell is broken, and another cycle begins:
binge and purge: indulgence without consequences
I think - until my acid-washed tonsils rebel and I'm 19
in the pediatric ward, recovering with jello
and ice cream (no less) and syrup sweet codeine
to lessen the pain.

Discharged, exercise replaces bulimia -
another attempt to control
my body, my image - seeking perfection -
always striving to be my mother, my brother, another.
Rigid allegiance to my self-imposed
regime: a dictator without discretion.

My 20s and 30s spent running away from myself
into music and television, the noise a distraction
from the void my dreams left when puberty arrived.
Finding comfort in fantasy and adrenaline,
in other people's struggles, followed by
withdrawals from Downton Abbey,
the end of basketball season, the last episode of Survivor.

Seeking my next fix, pink elephants push into the room,
filling its empty space, rearing on heavy hindquarters,
their pleather skin breaking out in a cold sweat of withdrawal.
Pain and change are a nicotine patch
on my spirit, my spirit emptied, lost.
Bone-shaking delirium, tremors
against the open places, seeking an edge,
seeking a boundary, a safe place, strait-jacketed.
Bouncing from one extreme to the other,
not knowing or wanting any middle ground.

Swaddled, disarmed and alarmed, I move
on to the next, high or low:
only stimulus or sleep can soothe,
no solace in purgatory, anything to avoid
confronting myself.

Side Effects

May cause:

Abnormal dreams
Denial
Delirium
Impotence
Coronary heart disease
Tremors
Insomnia
Organ failure
Night terrors

Call now for your free consultation!

CYNTHIA QUEVEDO

"Scandal"

It calls to me.
I try to work.
Its relentless call can
not go unanswered.'
There's a place in my soul
that it touches,
takes hold with its
creepy, spindle fingers.
They drag me to the television.
They hand me the remote.
They push the buttons
that bring the "Scandal" Netflix tile
to be highlighted and
then started.
That's it.
I'm in.
I'm hooked.
Next thing I know, I'm binge watching
two, sometimes three or four, episodes
before I can break away.
Break away to
live my life
wash and fold my laundry
cook my dinner
sleep.
As I write about "Scandal", it pulls at me,
but there's nowhere to watch. I'm safe.
For the moment.

G. MURRAY THOMAS

Recycling

I am cleaning all the old
beer bottles out of my garage.
It's been a couple of months,
there are quite a few of them,
a mound of green and brown
remnants of debauchery.
Some still have beer in them
(green moldy beer)
some have cockroaches
(they especially like Mickey's Big Mouth).
I dump them all out,
sort them,
load them into my
fuel-efficient car.

I drive to the recycling center
on the freeway. It is always crowded.
This is one rare time I feel justified
being there. This is one errand
I could not do on the bus,
even if there was one.
The curves of the brown hills
are diffused by the yellow sky
which slowly fades to one patch
of perfect blue
dead overhead.

The recycling center is crowded.
A street person with a shopping cart full of cans;
A mother with a little girl and
a station wagon full of newspapers;
an accountant with clean reams
of computer paper; a mechanic
looking for hubcaps;
and me with my beer bottles.

There are mountain ranges
of newspapers along the walls
and the endless crunch and clatter
of waste being ground up.
My cargo earns me $13.57.
I use it to buy
another case of beer.

JOSH JENNINGS WOOD

Prayer For My Mother

Drain the pool

Take everything out of the house—

the newspapers stacked like landmine skyscrapers, the mountain of
shoes crumbling out of the closet, the rows of jewelry caked in dust on
the dresser, the dresser overflowing with oversized t-shirts, drawers of
videocassettes labeled and unlabeled, the boots of car oil, phone books,
credit card offers, credit card bills, the crisp closet of uniform uniforms,
his safes, bottles of vodka, bottles of whiskey, bottles of tequila, his secret
safes, past tax statements, bundles of remote controls, vials of medicine
lining the cabinet like sharks teeth—

Take it all outside
Throw it in the pool
Soak it in gasoline
And burn it

JAIMES PALACIO

Mother

For my brother Luis and my sister Carmen
Clues stacked expectant, hidden
under the sink, in the kitchen
cabinet, empty and rolling on top
of the television, parading peacocks
of a tele-novela.-

Smiling faces in an open family scrapbook, like a movie
cut by studio and not director, missing
important chunks of story; as incongruous
as a phonebooth in a dessert.

Or at least as strange as mother
has become.

The stuttering train of memory runs
through the room junctioned by the dents
in the plaster where her fists gathered blood.

The broken mirrors are resigned to what
is reflected of her ghosts. Sent back in teams
from the scene of the crime.

Ripping false eyelashes off the faces
of strangers.

Flinging herself from moving vehicles in Tijuana.

Awake at 3 a.m. with the sudden desire to wash
someone's hair. Oblivious to cavalry or Calvary, disowning
daughter and sons on a whim, growling
into the phone:

"This is the last time you will hear from me.
You don't have a mother anymore."

Mother with the poisoned water.
Keeping the dead in the walls.
Standing by president's decisions
to drop bombs.

Mother missing.

Summoned by the Holy
Order of Black Labels into some hidden
wonderland where only her own
imperceptible language is spoken.

Meanwhile, the dutiful younger son throws
pennies into an alley in the hope
that others might find the luck
his family seems destined to avoid.

MAIA VILLA

always be

i am your baby girl,

      your baby gee,

you sing to me.

see my eyes. see light.

for me, you can be free.

i am a small hand that holds yours tight when there's a scary thing on tv.

i am a tree branch stretching out above your quicksand; hold onto me.

i will grow into a woman who will trace my thumb against your brow when you feel lonely.

i will grow, as long as you grow with me.

a little girl does not want to see her daddy, back cemented to the ground, hand reaching for bottle already empty.

i love you.

please.

reach for me.

This Gun is Real

I have seen my face in the black metal
felt the heat
breathed gray dust hanging
in the air.

This kid knows
what makes Saturday night special.

I open the flue
hide the gun in the chimney.

I am talking about terror.

Now I look for the knife.
this knife is real.
I have seen it at work
slicing the Sunday roast.

I slide the knife
into the shoe box
replace the lid.

Now it's the middle of the night.
I am lying on the floor.
From the light under my door
two voices.

He says, "I'm taking the kid."
She says, "I'll do anything."

Something black comes up from my stomach
covers me.
This child knows
how to die.

Sundays he sleeps late.
We get up early.
I bring her the knife.
She starts dinner.

His favorite
pot roast sliced thin
pearly white onions
potatoes steamed in their pink jackets

leftovers all week.

From *Traveler in Paradise: New and Selected Poems,* PEARL Editions, 2004

MAIA VILLA

simmer

How much longer will I boil before
She lifts the lid? A pot left be will dry.
One burst from I she will recoil before
She dare look in mine eye. Oh, maiden once
Fair, I accept the scars cracklin' beneath
Thine estranged steps. Still, if only thou had
Thought of me when thou first thought of him.

Stumbled into long corridor, I fall
Into dark chamber. Hit by the white of
His still eye, my body's sent to thunder.
"Get out! Get out! Get out!" I scream, yet still
he rests in her bed. Why will he not let
me be? Why must he rest too in my head?
She lifts, breasts full in open blouse. She looks
at me as though I make no sound. I scream
Again, and then I understand: Cords tugged
By choking puffs of air, no sounds I have.

I cannot always wake so helplessly
In muffled uproar, pillows drowning. Much
Better spent mine dreams would be if left in
Longing for man deceased. So if thou please,
Free me.

How much longer would I have boiled before
Man deceased would have lifted the lid? A pot left be will dry.
One burst from I would he have recoiled,
Or looked in mine eye? Oh, Great King,
Once hero, I accepted the scars cracklin' between
Thine fingertips. Still, if only thou had
Thought of me before thou took thine
Noxious sip.

Cradled in father-daughter cove, I melt
in love and laughter. Hit by the

tickle-finger-buddy, my body's sent into child's thunder.
"Shoopy, Shoopy, I love you..." He mewls, he clasps
Me tightly. "Promise me, you'll always love me,
You'll always call me daddy."
Phone rings. Silence fills the house. He walks
Away from me, an unfamiliar man now. I cradle myself
Alone. Our cove is just a couch. My little finger
Traces the bumpy texture; into the phone, he growls...
"You fuck fuh-fucking bitch. Fucking whore. You fuh-fuh-fucking
bitch."

I sit in the backseat of Mom's car, and
I don't understand. Eyes pierced, I say to her,
"We were happy before you called.
I wish you'd left me with
-- Dad."

Present day: I cannot fall for a guy who stains beer to his lips,
Even if he makes the hair on my neck rise with his fingertips.
Much better spent our days would be
healing from the upbringing
that brought you and me
here.
So if you please,
Leave me.
Be free,
from the memories still haunting.
"Mai, sometimes it's just the timing."
But if you're ever to call me,
Remember, dream lover,
Simmer gently.

DONNA HILBERT

1942 Snapshot of my Father

He could be my child,
this boy at seventeen,
centered in front of a palm tree
in the parkway
of his sister's yard.
This motherless kid,

in a borrowed sports coat
and slacks that fold
too deeply over his shoes.
His curly hair is combed back.
His lips part in an almost grin.

I know the history of this picture:
how he came to California to find work.
How he dug ditches, riveted metal,
picked fruit,
returned to Oklahoma to marry his girl
before he turned eighteen. Nothing

to remark about, given the war.
And I know the life that followed:
the guns hidden in chimneys, bruises
under scarves, how the half-smile
concealed a boozy rage. Still,

it moves me:
how he glistens in this picture,
the deep crease of his slacks,
his boyish curls.

From *Traveler in Paradise: New and Selected Poems*, PEARL Editions, 2004

CHRISSIE MORRIS BRADY

Best

A shy skinny Irish lad
Homesick for his neighborhood
Never caused trouble
Talented and promising

Two years later
We called him Superstar
The first since Jesus Christ
Sideburns, girls, fame

Feet like fingers of a pickpocket
His left as good as his right
He would leave his opponents
With their blood twisted

Ten years he shone
A star, a supernova
He had class, a gift
True charisma

Then he got bored with girls
So moved on the drink
Gambling and women
Ennui took him

Ten years he shone
A moon out of the night
And twenty years
He took to die

No more magic dribbling the ball
Just famous for drinking
Shooting star lost in black holes
Pitied, shamed, wasted

BETSY MARS

Music from a Farther Room

A lost soul, set in his ways,
a haze of indecisions and revisions -
like a young Prufrock, his hopes
receding like his hairline.
Ambition and intelligence no longer aligned.
His mind a fast current, a rogue wave
threatening to drag him out to sea.

He recoils at the shoreline.
Hesitant, he ages, his summer fruit
left spoiling upon the tree:
his body an empty husk, weighted down
by the wet sand ballasts
rolled in the trouser cuffs of his dusty dreams.

The way ahead no longer clear, a blurry line,
the end always slightly out of reach, slightly out of mind.
He'd beseech the empty heavens to dislodge
the universal despair that, insidious,
cloaks his brain, should he dare.

There will be time, always time -
ticking time bombs of the buried past,
left with nothing but siren songs at last
to call him back from the precipice
of painful memories reflected
in the distorting mirror of his muddled mind.

Genetics and circumstances:
a reverse alchemy of the two,
turn the golden child to lead.
Thoughts cryptic and incessant
scramble for dominance in his head.
His resources, finite, are strained past bearing.
His etherized brain is long past caring.

Paralyzed by lethargy and liquor -
his toxic toast and tea -
each choice a momentary cure for the illness
of intolerable sobriety.

The mermaids sing still upon the distant rocks;
he sleeps sated upon the floor, breathing, ragged,
muttering but not malingering. Seeking refuge,
his thoughts scuttle across the rocky sea
bottom of his crumpled universe.

In time he shall emerge from his gray chamber.
The sand now dry will trickle through the open weave.
Lightened, this steep hill he shall conquer,
and unburdened, take his waking leave.

DONNA HILBERT

Madeleine

I think of you lying on the couch,
days after the birth of our boy—
your grandson—how your sobs
awakened me from fitful sleep
that first morning home.
You'd come to care for me, the baby,
your bewildered son.
Between the tears you said that no one loved you,
and now, surrounded by all this life,
you felt still more alone.
I watched you cry
as if watching a foreign movie,
in a language I couldn't speak.
I searched for meaning in what I saw:
your hair the color of bourbon
in the almost empty bottle
beside you on the floor.
I watched your face, still beautiful
un-mottled, smooth.
But I listened un-moved,
while you complained that I failed
to appreciate all you'd done—
marigolds planted by the back door,
the freshly laundered sheets.
Later, fueled by still more bourbon,
you started a fire
drying socks on the old gas stove.
I told your son to send you home
or I would take the baby and go.
Deep in my fertile life
I couldn't fathom such unhappiness,
didn't know the other meaning of passion,
had no language for such hunger,
had no language for such grief.

from *The Green Season*, World Parade Books, 2009

CLIFTON SNIDER

The Day Elvis Died

I

He was Assembly of God,
I an Assembly of God preacher's kid.
Dad denounced his music
from the pulpit in Terre Haute, Indiana,
played a sample, compared it
to church music.

I missed him on Ed Sullivan:
we had church on Sunday nights.
His music penetrated the air waves
on the radio and TV. He softened
his critics with gospel recordings.

I thought his voice weak on
"Love Me Tender," strong
on "Hound Dog." Then came
the army and the movies
(I saw none of them) and
his electric, black leather clad
comeback on TV, his sexy
rock and roll charisma
born again
as if it were never gone.

Fat Elvis breezed through Albuquerque
when I was in grad school there.
Somehow I missed my last chance
to see him.

II

I walk home from the beach
to my upstairs apartment,
Long Beach, 16 August 1977.

The cute sailor next door
appears on the balcony,
tells me Elvis Presley has died.

I'm dead tired from teaching
remedial English, hung over,
four hours every morning
at the local community college.

The radio & TV stations play
almost exclusively one song,
"Are You Lonesome Tonight,"
between the known details
of his dying, as if it were
his most representative
& appropriate song,
with his melodramatic
spoken voice about the world
as a stage where love is lost,
a poignant interlude,
an introduction to the grave.

Drunk that I am,
a year before sobriety,
I attempt to save the moment,
record from the radio
on my cassette tape recorder
till it jams while I am passed out.

Next morning, head throbbing,
dehydrated, drained,
I face a room of domestic
& foreign students.
They don't mind that I play
what I could save from my tape:
"Are You Lonesome Tonight."

RAUNDI MOORE-KONDO

A Crooked Sidewalk Followed Me Home

There are no straight and narrows to follow. No extra credit for good behavior, regular attendance or for turning oneself in or around. Memories are short. No one remembers the good deeds performed yesterday. They will only remember how fucked up I was tonight. And how late I will be tomorrow.

Tonight a crooked sidewalk followed me home. Ghosting me. Lurking under every step. Sometimes coming up short, other times coming up too quick. Yet all the while, staying true to the destination. Meeting the paces of my stumblings in what science tells me is always the equal

and opposite direction. Often switching back on myself I gave birth to one complex, sorry-assed excuse for a trail that longed to be a vomitless path. It became about just keeping up. Moving along. Forward march. Running requires less deliberation. Except Running feels more like being

chased. Like harassment, because no one's timing me. No one's expecting me. No one knows where I am, or where I aim to go. Except for the sidewalk. No matter which way I turn, my feet can't escape the ground. And gravity can make for one hell of a hostile work environment.

Rabbits escape some predators with indiscriminate zigzagged getaways. Running the pursuant ragged. It's in the turnouts that too much energy is expended. Braking at break neck speeds and sprinting while high on adrenaline. The more desperate and stubborn sometimes chase themselves to death.

This planet is toying with me. Insidiously wearing me down. Shifting and quaking underfoot. If for no other reason than to force me to concentrate, so I'll stay on my feet. Prodding me on. Reminding me that I can't spend another night sleeping in the street.

I made it. Home had never taken so many awkward steps to get to. Sometimes nothing feels better than a doorknob in my hand, no matter how hard I worked to get there.

JONATHAN YUNGKANS

Coffee

Morning coaxes, cold
one cup and thought

at a time from bones.
No milk or sugar

but undiluted quiet
from a stove's burners,

a phantom clock
once on a white wall

above my chair
and the black comfort

that calls remembrance
past a red eye,

brewing
through the dullness,

regrets and missed lives.
I turn to it

for warmth
on days only it touch me.

We are so alike—
cooling, then tepid,

left with a dark ring
and spent grounds.

Window Strikes

Like faked-out birds
we slammed into one another's reflections,
passed out on kitchen linoleum
and drooled until morning sun
split our heads awake.

We paid penance of instant coffee
laced with bourbon
and pancake batter browned in beer,
pretended to job hunt the classifieds
of yesterday's stolen paper,
disconnected phone calls
to end the breakfast charade.

Hair of dog quelling stomach flu
we showered with the passion of young lovers;
became the couple we were meant to be,
tumbling on stained sheets
arching upright against the window,
laughing at the traffic below.

No neighbors would interfere
as the last of our dishes clattered
and our squawking echoed.
Romance only lasted a while
before keeping up with our "Jones"
became our mission,
to score drugs again our only cause
as we blame-gamed one-another
for our sorry-ass condition.

Originally published in *On Summer Solstice Road* by Jerry Garcia ©2016

MURRAY THOMAS

The Morning After

The room reeked of stale poetry.
There was poetry spilled all over the carpet.
The kitchen counter was covered with aluminum cans
    half full of warm poetry
    with cigarette butts floating in it.
And my head ached
    with that particular sharp pain
    that only comes from worn out neurons
    abused with too much imagined brilliance
    inspired by an excessive consumption
    of poetry.
So I sat down and
    - what else -
    cracked open a cold poem.

JERRY GARCIA

Ten Sunday mornings later,

corner of Cahuenga and Vine
newspaper man hawking headlines.

Drooped across cement lines
your dancewear
smudged and greasy
panty hose
shredded
caked in homeless grime,
heels busted.

Corroding like the handle
of your rusted vanity mirror
you clutch a Styrofoam cup
full of coins
from Samaritans walking
toward their redemption.

Church bells thump
in the distance.

Originally published in *On Summer Solstice Road* by Jerry Garcia © 2016

PEGGY CARTER

Memory

The page holds your words
they stare up into my face
and I remember

how good it was to talk to you
how we shared our thoughts on
our blank pages

I need to shred those words
I know I do
but now you're back
in my life
with every emotion I felt

I cannot do this thing.
To shred those words means tearing at myself –
at my deep longing
for your presence here

I gaze into the abyss where you have gone
and I know the words are all I have left
from you –

Why have you gone away –

JENNIFER BRADPIECE

Real

You write...
Perhaps you like to think you start with wood.
Perhaps you start with wood and then you chisel the eyes,
wide enough for detail, but narrow cornered, so as not to take in
too much light.
Then a nose, for specific scents only.
Two secret lips that might speak.
You want the wood to live and breath; you want it real.

Perhaps you think the magic dust that makes it real is vodka or
cocaine.
Maybe you think it's speed or Xanax or sex with strangers.
Or maybe it's the cigarettes or the angle the light hits the wall
across from you.

And maybe it is sex with strangers.
But maybe it is sex with yourself.
Maybe the poem is sex and you are the stranger.
Maybe the poem is stranger than you.
Maybe the poem is real.
Maybe the poem is more real than the event it recalls.
Maybe the event the poem is based on only feels real on the
page, as a poem.

Maybe that's when you realize that you life is the wood
and you and your psychiatrist have
very different ideas
about
what makes wood real.

First published in *Media Cakes*

AUSTYN GUTHRIE

More

I have more
Lines than stanzas
And I write
Everyday

Everyday, I feel
I have more
So I write
More lines than stanzas

Why don't I do it,
By doing it?
I have more
Would you like a read?

Feel free to explore
I do this everyday
My drawers are full
And I have more

MIKE LEMP

Loving Addiction

I love writing little poems about things with truth or fiction.
But I am starting to feel that it has become a strong addiction.
When someone mentions a specific and it happens all the time.
I find myself occupied and searching for words that rhyme.
I have talked with several people and I'm becoming very sure.
That it's a permanent addiction and I'll never find a cure.
But if you think you have a cure that would really help me quit.
I hope you will not tell me, because I'm sure enjoying it.

ELLYN MAYBE

Addiction Subtraction

A diction. A dictionary.

Speaking through a hole in the soul.

MARC CID

A Happier Ending

I am addicted to murder mysteries, and other stories
where there are people dedicated towards uncovering
the truth behind a death, people who flash badges
to ask questions of surviving friends, family, coworkers,
neighbors, to glean secondhand fragments of the dead.
In these stories, detectives and investigators are driven
by curiosity, by a sense of justice, by a desire
to uncover murderer motive, asking
what was your relationship to the victim,
was she acting strangely in the days leading up
to her death, is there anyone
who would want her dead?

I am addicted to tactical role playing games.
Maybe it's because they portray the way failure
is always a possibility, but one reducible by teamwork,
the way all heroes have vulnerabilities,
compensated by the support of their friends,
how their plots depict revolutions starting small, sputtering
and stuttering, little more than bluster and hot blood,
and how the seeds of tyranny can sprout back up at any time,
how good people sometimes pick the wrong side to fight for,
how comrades in arms can disagree
on what a right side would be shaped like,
and how abruptly and unexpectedly
a hero can be isolated by the enemy
from a sudden pile-up of hasty actions,
because such games play like chess,
where every piece possesses
strengths and weaknesses, recognizing
that isolation will kill even a queen.
Maybe it's the subtitles of these games:
Save the Light
Absence of Justice

Devil Survivor
Let Us Cling Together
We'll Never Fight Alone

I am addicted to fictions and simulations
of life. It is nothing more than escapism,
nothing more than abject denial
of everything I learned at your funeral and after.
No one was investigating.
They were telling stories:
bright stories, springtime stories
denial stories, whitewash stories,
if she was really as happy as you say
then why did she kill herself stories.

The pastors told a story too.
A story of a girl who had no name,
who through God's grace survived
her fall for a little while longer,
long enough to be driven to the ER,
long enough for her family to arrive,
long enough for her to ask God
for forgiveness for amazing grace
how sweet the sound that saved
a wretch like her who spurred
the gift of life she didn't deserve
that none of us deserve they sang at her service.
A story where by the grace of God she lingered
long enough to tell her brother
she was sorry, she jumped because
she was angry at her father
who shed tears as so many churchgoers
who had never spoken to her
offered their condolences to him
except no, they didn't tell that part.
That part is a deleted scene.
The test audience did not respond well.

They demanded a happier ending.

JONATHAN YUNGKANS

Point Vincente

Charcoal clouds twist and call,
braid squalls above the lighthouse
and the roil between my ears
that says I won't drown,
break isn't smash, isn't sound

but finally quiet. I swing,
tied to this cliff's rope noose
and the effervescent lie that is only light—
a day of filaments
woven between ingoing and outgoing,
rolling to a rest rollers wash.

A sign on the rail
either calls for responsible suicide
or an attempt at Palos Verdes humor:
"Set A Positive Example:
Don't Even Try It."
The writer must've known too well

what Williams called the sea's sadness,
how its undertow catches
till you can't live without it or can't live.
Words break across steel pipes
in desires more vivid than memory.

JAIMES PALACIO

Insomnia

God,
there he is, at it again, the man with the hole
in his head is having sick conversations with
the ceiling, contemplating the etymology
of words. Insomnia is an addiction he can't
break. The path of planets is crowing his
ineffectuality. "Oh, were you just dreaming?"
He had that re-occurring encounter with
the sharks. They wanted his dictionary.
Wanted to warn him that his hair was
thinning, that his chances of surviving
a date or finding a job are diminishing
with every wrong move. Every missed step.
He thinks he knows the microscopic
trembles of rope breaking the neck. Often
has thought "How easy it would be."
To let the wheels slip. To find the right
vein. To drown in the depths of oceans, the
crawling vastness of space looking for
that all encompassing "Always" But he
is only still dreaming, finding variations
of ceilings. Night holds rejection well, fits
like the treacherous smile on a Great White, like
the way arms bend out to receive the coming
sunrise or a crucifixion.

CHRISTINE ISHERWOOD

Rotten

here i am again
encountering death
which has been sneaking up
inside me
for a very long time.
my shadow death,
my unconscious self,
teetering on the edge of the precipice
while gaily telling everyone
i am ok,
no, don't worry about me.

death calls me in,
lures me with its magical songs,
eats me up,
but because i stoppered my ears
with wax
i thought i was immune
to the sweet, sweet tunes
it crooned.

oh death, why do you dance with me so,
death, why do you crave me so,
death, why do you haunt my doorstep,
court me through so many years,
and tell me i will be yours,
if not now, then soon.
for i have aligned myself with a desire for life,
but still you caught me in your net,
i was so sick, and i did not know.

the trees showered me with petals,
a skeleton of love that remained
when all else was gone.
and like a love lost,

parts of it splintered,
broke off,
and were swept away by the tide.
you snagged my dark side,
grabbed it in terrier teeth, and snarling and
gnarling you clung on and on to the shadows,
until you proclaimed that day was night,
that dark was light and all there was was rotten.
rotten.
rotten to the core,
rotten,
what a whore,
rotten like a lying, thieving, disreputable,
unloved, untrustworthy piece of nothing.
like a tangled rotting star,
mangled,
manacled and decayed.

here, on the island of bones,
no one knows the terrible things i am.
here on the beach,
here i beseech,
here let me love and lay down.
as the sun sets and life begets
another round of reasoning.
days go by, horses fly,
i weep, yet weep, yet weep.
yet i weep and sing,
despite what the day brings,
and bones and blossoms
and grace from above.

JAIMES PALACIO

Why I Share In The Frustration Of The Young Lady And Her Earnest Contemplation Of War

Because we are having a call and response
with houseplants high on chlorophyll and Vivaldi.

Because the president on the television just lied.
Because the president on the television lies a lot.

Because "MY GOD, DID YOU SEE THAT?!"
Because "YES, I DID BUT WHAT CAN WE DO?"

Because I'm being pulled like Ahab or the captain in the
alternate version of Jaws.

Getting the bends.

Drowning in headlines.

Choking from the ash in the fine lines.

Because the tombstone industry is having a good year!
Because victim's movements are no longer parallel
with Earth's gravitation.

Because the night is a long fist!
Because the day is a hot tar!

Because my bellow is echo!
Because my scream is useless!

Because the ozone is growing fangs!
Because mother nature has turned vigilante!

Because the universe is expanding!
Because light is false!

Because I can't see the light!
Because there is no light!

Because a young lady is on stage and juggling "Why's"
like refrigerators filled with bowling balls!
Because I can see the victims!
Because they are shattered mirrors of themselves!

Because the Captains and the Generals and the Majors are all
junkies.
Because war is the ultimate addiction and the Dorito headed
president on the television is stoned
out of his mind.

Because sadly, a young lady's questions mean as much to all of
them now
as Vivaldi means to house plants.

Because there is always just the restless
wind of memory whispering: "Why?"

JOSH JENNINGS WOOD

Freedom is Free

I'd like to take the 9-11 hijackers
& get them all high & give them Doritos
I'd like to drop acid with Rush Limbaugh
Pat Robertson & some Sudanese
warlords and watch *Houses of the Holy*
Listen to that, man. Look at those *cobwebs*
I'd like to hot box Saudi Arabia
Cruise through the supermarket's bright midnight
in sunglasses, giggling at the ice cream
freezer buzz with the Grand Wizard & crew

Because the happiest I've ever been
was in high school, riding beside my brother
too high to do anything but smile, too high
to know anything could ever be wrong

I'd like to strip. Here. For you. I mean it. Strip:
like the prisoners in that human pyramid
like the prisoners in that rape basement
like the prisoners dead in custody
like the prisoners in her own bedrooms

DERRICK ORTEGA

Turnaround Trip

Ingie had a great idea to head to vegas with a car full of minorities
and a bag full of party and a tank full of gas and we decided to drop
the hookah hoses and exhale the double apple smoke into the arabic
language lingering in the air like billion year old stardust and we got up
from our posh plush mush brush crushed red velvet couches and ran to
his teeny tiny two door sedan like little boys and girls running after a
tip top ice cream truck with bombpops and push pops and strawberry
topped goodness so we can nest ourselves in the cheap seats of his
japanese with our american knees criss crossed apple sauce this wont
cost us a dime a dozen of dollars in our pockets with a bag of party with
the crystals with the can do attitude we thought we had we thought we
have we thought we will have in vegas in the city of lights where the goat
of mendes secretly hides on the tops of decks of cards looking face up
as bar bar bar hits and strikes and gongs the electronic bells over and
over and over as elderly people are given shiny pretty cheery coins that
make them smile that make them fuzzy that make them have an eternal
moment of winning before the casino dust pans sweep up their ashes and
their leftovers and their buffet credits with their club cards shredded with
the credit cards denied on funds that losers and boozers and schmoozers
and floozies and doozies in this anonymous autonomous get fond of this
lifestyle we are about to embark upon onto into between the cracks of
the heads of the crackheads that stroll down the strip to strip so they can
keep strolling down our way his way her way their way every way a person
can make a dollar so they can buy their fix even if it comes in the form of a
bill or a pillow or a powder or a fluid that takes the form of a soft ethereal
empyreal very real spiritual featherfilled flying across the socal deserts
where the water and the rotted and the bothered flooded the emptiness
that shouldnt be nested where birds cant even live and cant even raise
their unhatched midget copies of themselves that would crack the egg
and protrude their necks for chopped vomit fed by mother who is just
going to push them out of the nest whether theyre ready or not to accept
this complex thrown against the wall of my life and your life and our life
what even is life until it sticks idea only to crust and fall to ashes to dust
to cinder to refuse to smut to granules to grime and grit and ground like
human bodies are meant to do by god by allah by yahweh by moloch

by vishnu by krishna by huwa by satnam by brahma by rama by dallas by bernie by tino by tuna by lenny by ingie by i am who am what am where am when am why am how am i going to handle the party with the pressure in the place with the people and the proper words to represent the right ideas i want everybody to get about someone who aint even eighteen yet.

RAUNDI MOORE-KONDO

Policy Changes

To whomever it may concern:

Please refer to the post-it note stuck to the underside
of my forehead which clearly states that from now on
anything less than "Euphoria" should be filed under
the heading labeled "PAIN" and medicated immediately.

Recent developments have been linked to a variety of causes:

Political pundits point their fingers at my
lobbyists who lobby against other lobbyists.
The head of the fed blames my sluggish economy
on my poorly-regulated, regulatory committees.
The military labeled all damages as collateral and
acceptable and will continue to colonize territory
without concern for friendly fire. Scientists hypothesize
over the questionable gene pool. Dopamine deficiencies,
are disregarded due to the lack of a controllable
control group. And now they only ponder what color
pills I might like best. The new pathways being formed
will deepen synapses, but will continue to make
the familiar less defined.

We apologize for any inconveniences during reconstruction:

You see, at one point in history
all my continents used to connect
with jigsaw puzzle precision.
A fit so tight, that no amount
of enlightenment dared to slip through.

Back then I bathed in one giant sea
warmed by magma and stirred
by a single satellite.
Borders hadn't been invented.

There had never been an apparent need
for that kind of bureaucracy.

Due to some sort of shift in tectonics
I find that I am all in pieces—
just a bunch of lawless Islands
drifting about like aimless ice floes.

Continually crashing into each other,
and sinking any ships who seek safe-passage
through these waters.

In conclusion the management is hopeful
the new filing system will simplify matters;
keep all departments on task
and from killing each other.

HARLAN WALLNER

Altered.

What is it to be addicted?
Hooked. Stuck. Trapped.
To continue using a substance or
behavior even though it causes
significant and worsening problems
in one's life.

The hungry ghost.
To be compelled to continue,
almost frantically, even when one
wants to stop.

Hello, my name is America and I'm an addict.

Even though it causes so many problems in my life
I just can't get enough oil.
I always want more mono-cropped
industrial agriculture.
I can't stop running the human children
through factory-system schools
where they are unnaturally classed and graded;
so often bullied, ridiculed,
traumatized, and shamed;
their creativity converted to conformity.
I can't stop using industrialized healthcare
even though, because it focuses almost explicitly
on reducing or eliminating symptoms
rather than addressing root causes
and imbalances (because those are usually systemic),
now more than 200,000 humans die of
iatrogenic causes each year—
that is, they die of something they didn't have
before they went to a doctor. Even though
so many human poor can't afford the
astronomical and growing expenses of
being seen by a healer when they are sick

or dying.
And I can't stop using punishment
as a means of altering the humans behavior
—fuck, <drool>
that one's my favorite—
even though it really only makes things worse;
even though the main thing it teaches
is not to do that thing in front of a
parent/teacher/authority,
and to be more careful not to get caught next time,
and to mistrust authority,
and to want to fight back;
even though it only creates more
arbitrary pain in the world
I use as much punishment as I can,
internally and with other countries.

I can't stop, I need my fix, I need
more rare earth metals for my tech
more Bangladeshi sweat shops for my textiles
more slaves,
more women forced into sex work
more cars
more houses
more strip malls
more pipelines
more wars
more prisons
more guns
more escapes
more pain relief
more ways to keep doing
all the things I've been doing
more ways to numb out and avoid
the horrors of my childhood.
I mean, how do I come to terms with
the attempted genocide of the
humans and cultures that populated
my landmass
before I was named America?
The enslavement and centuries of

horrifically violent mistreatment
of so many of the humans of Africa?
How do I come to peace with the
centuries of destructive and self-destructive
behavior, the trauma I've inflicted on others and
my own national-landscape-body?
I tell myself—and everybody who will listen—
that I'm the greatest that ever was,
but subconsciously, you know,
I can't believe that—
not after what I've done.
Not with all the festering sores I've acquired
over my centuries of use:
the superfund pollution sites
the rampant homelessness
the crime- and poverty-riddled inner cities
the overflowing prisons
the human addiction epidemic
(as above so below, right?)
the war veterans addicted, imprisoned, or
living on the streets
the spilled oil
the superweeds
the superbugs
the suicide epidemic...

And what the fuck can I even do?
Where does a nation go for rehab?
In humans, it's been found that seventy to
ninety percent of those addicted
relapse after rehab.
What hope is there for me?
I may as well continue using, right?
In humans, the physical structure of
the brain is changed by long term use
in ways that make normal functioning
very difficult without the substance.
In me, shit, just look at me.
My national landscape and culture-scape
has been so altered
that I don't remember how to live,

I don't know how to even function anymore
without cars, oil, schools, HMOs,
industrialized ag, the military-industrial-prison complex
big-box stores
electricity
mass-media
refrigeration.
Few of these things even existed
when I was born, but now I'm so dependent on them
untold millions of my humans would
probably just die without them.

Not only that, but *I've been the pusher*
on the global scene.
I've been the dealer,
I've been roughing up
everybody not as tough as me,
starting banana wars and
drug wars and oil wars,
shit, I've wiped entire cultures off the globe,
eradicated entire languages.
How I can I turn soft now?

And I *know* that my habits are killing me.
I *know* disaster is coming,
that there's a rock-bottom lurking
in my future, that anything
"unsustainable" can only go on
for so long before it collapses,
and I know that
at this point my rock-bottom may be
six feet under.
I *know* this, because I have so many human scientists
looking deeply at the impacts of
my behavior, but I'm scared shitless to really admit it.
I know, but still
I can't stop. I can't let down the facade.
I don't even know how
and I'm terrified of trying.
I don't even know who I am anymore
without all my fixes.

So I keep repeating my old shtick:
I'm the greatest that ever was
and my way is the right way
and if you mess with me I'm gonna
fuck you up.

But I'll tell you a secret:
I really want to stop.
I hate this way of life,
I hate all the rushing around,
I hate all the pain it's causing.
I'm so tired of hurting myself and
other nations, species, cultures, peoples,
ecosystems, rivers, and our mother earth.
It may be hard to believe but, on some level
it's all been a screaming, wailing,
grasping cry for help,
a desperate reaching for
relief from the pain.

Maybe you can find a way to help me?
I know that if the rubric of justice that
my courts apply to humans were
to be applied to me after all the
aggression, flagrant ecological despoliation,
genocidal acts, and economic violence I've
inflicted on other nations, I would receive
incredibly harsh punishment,
in fact, I'd probably scream for the
death penalty myself if an individual human
inflicted even a minuscule fraction
of the harm I've inflicted over the
span of my relatively short life.
But what if the conventions of
punishment are flawed and ineffectual,
the misguided product of an addiction?
I still deserve compassion,
don't I?

PEGGY DOBREER

Intervention

America should to go to rehab,
should not pass go, not
collect one more red-cent
from the ninety-nine. America
could crash and burn, lives in
terror, kicking and punting, and
shooting bloody murder. America
should go to rehab, but she said no.

America, *man*, has plenty much cash
on hand to feed her habit, oily and
fractual, she will steal from our babies,
books & meds, leave them hungry,
in squalor, on streets, in gutters, no pencils
for school, face down and fed up, latch key,
distended, and distant, and distant, and
more and more distant.

America should pull herself off the corner,
put down her profits, go to rehab. What
other choice does she have but destruction?
America is addicted to her wealth but won't
come clean, won't spend of the wind,
hyped on greed fed by a need to subjugate,
and bring our lady of no liberty to her knees.

Long forgotten is first vision of fore fathers
who occupied from stolen indigeny. Founded
on freedoms that wring out atrocities.
America is already under scrutiny by
the fat arm of karma and each global eye
once keened on these glittering shores.

America is covered in tracks
but no one wants to see. No one

will admit to the bruising. No one
can stop her, rein her, turn her. No
one percent. America needs to go
to rehab not kicking and scratching,
not whining and moaning. But take
her singing, signing, and resisting,
ninety-nine times ninety-nine,
times ninety-nine.

CANDEE WILDE-KONDO

I Cannot Forget This Number

BJ5692484. BJ5692484. B.J.5.6.9.2.4.8.4.

This sequence of numbers rolls through my head every day, over and over. Some days, hundreds of times. I hear it set to a little tune that I do not recognize. I see it when I close my eyes sometimes, as if repetition has left it burned onto the inside of my forehead. I cannot forget this number. I have tried.

Typically, I am not good at remembering numbers. I do not remember my old addresses and have been known to take a noticeable second to think of my current phone number if I have not used it for a while. Although I am a decade away from collecting benefits and my memory is otherwise adequate, I have to run through my entire Social Security number to come up with the last four digits. I have never had a head for numbers.

So I was surprised when I decided to use this number a second time and realized I knew it by heart. I was sitting at my husband's desk in our study, feeling jangly with adrenalin. Or maybe it was opiate withdrawal that was making me sweat lightly. I had already written the date on the prescription form, and my name and date of birth.

The middle section was finished too. MS Contin 100mg, #90 tablets. I had indicated 'zero' next to refills, because the Drug Enforcement Administration does not allow narcotic prescriptions to be refilled. I was careful to fill it out exactly as my pain management doctor wrote it for me.

I already had signed my husband's name on the prescription, but I had not tried to forge it. That was a point of pride with me. I knew I would be caught eventually, and when it happened, I think the state and federal DEA agents went easier on me in their reports because I had taken this small step to avoid implicating my husband. I used his prescription blanks several times a month for nearly two years, but I did not try to copy his signature exactly.

Unfortunately, this nod at honor was lost on my husband as he fought to retain the DEA license that allowed him to practice anesthesiology. I live in a different state now but as far as I know, he still has the same number.

CHRISTINE ISHERWOOD

Anaesthia

All I can do
is hope
and
resist the numbness of sleep,
ward off the carriers of anesthesia,
deny them my soul,
decline, decline, decline
their kind invite.

No! No! do not approach,
stay away
for I am trying my best
to stay awake and
not be tempted by noxious poisons
and bites of fancy food injected with
sleeping sickness and
all I can do is dream
and hope
and sleep
and wake
and be
and sing
and dance
and breathe
and write
and urge myself
to remain awake,
to not fall into a soul's slumber,
to not forget,
no, never forget.
All I can do
is hope
and live
and dream.
All I can do.

Meanwhile,
my heart is fluttering away
like a little frightened bird.
I cannot try enough,
and the river flows fast at my feet.

DEANNE MEEKS BROWN

Transformation

Hungry for love

I bit into the forbidden fruit

Hungry to be whole

I ate the entire enchilada

Hungry to be still

I drank from cool waters

Hungry for clarity I

Swallowed a bag of diamonds

And cut them into stars

RAUNDI MOORE-KONDO

An Addicts Thriving Guide

I.
Collect a lot of addictions: As many as you possibly can. Variety is key.
Mix them up at will. Make them all seem recreational, unrehearsed--an
after thought. Probably just a stay-cation left-over. Nothing more than a
little random act of kindness to ones self.

II.
Embrace all the logical and natural consequences as valuable learning
experiences; further rationalization may never be required. If all else fails,
label yourself an artist.

III.
Improvisation is a gift bestowed upon those who can't stop acting: And,
to those who refuse to stop dancing long enough to learn the steps- Fuck
choreography but never react. Become a non-stop, in the moment, risk-
analysis machine. Be prepared to make spur of the moment, good-faith
deals with dust devils and dirty dishes for the promise of a solid and shiny
soul.

IV.
Never underestimate the importance of damage control: Look busy. Learn
to use algorithms and psychoanalysis to actualize best-case scenarios and
create diversions. Forge ahead with your worst decisions and greatest
intentions. Never ask for permission, but be prepared to apologize.

V.
Enable your enablers.

P.S. I wore this just for you. I'll never wear it for anyone, but you. Tomorrow
when I burn it, neither of us will know exactly what it meant.

ANGELA MOORE

INTRODUCING LIFE, THE BOARD GAME: ADDICTION EDITION!

Good for as many players as we can get, and thanks to those working so diligently to provide drugs to everyone (prescription or otherwise), this game is available to everyone from birth to death.

SET UP

- Choose your token: a wine glass, syringe, Rx vial, etc. You say you're not an addict? Not to worry, we provide tokens for the codependents of the game: a hero's cape, jester's marotte, martyr's whip, etc.

- Separate the cards: The Circumstance deck contains cards such as race, socio-economic status, mental health status, etc. The Event deck contains cards such as "Neighbor calls 911 about your after-hours party." The Public Policy deck contains cards such as "City council increases police presence in and around schools."

- Draw three cards from the Circumstance deck.

GAME PLAY

- Player with the most privileged circumstances goes first.

- Roll the dice and move your token, then pick a card from the deck indicated.

EXAMPLES

- Pick an Event card that states "Fail DUI test during traffic stop." Your Circumstance cards will determine your next step: Your race card may get you sent to the morgue (game over for you), or sent home with a warning (you may move on your next turn). Your socio-economic status card may get you sent to jail (skip next three turns), or to a rehabilitation facility (skip next turn only).

- Pick a Public Policy card that states "VA health services funding reduced." Again, your Circumstance cards determine what's next: Your health status card may allow you to move forward to a licensed health practitioner, or backward to an illicit drug dealer.

- Pick a Circumstance card and stay where you are. It will help determine your future moves.

During the game you will end up in at least one of the following corners:

- Prison, probation, unemployment, prison. Chances are slim that you'll pick a card that will release you from the cycle.
- Rehab, working a program, relapse, rehab. Keep going in circles unless you pick a card that breaks this cycle.
- Recovery: setting boundaries, enforcing said boundaries when tested, replacing coping mechanisms. Warning: you may draw a card that sets you back.

GAME END

The Morgue is the fourth and final corner: you can die during the game due to overdose, medical malpractice (such as misdiagnosing the underlying cause of substance abuse), incarceration (such as refusal to provide medical treatment due to prison privatization), etc.

Game is over when the last player dies.

ACKNOWLEDGEMENTS

John Gardiner for our epic title from his poem *Junkie Blues*, Savanah Kondo for editing and graphic design, the poets of Southern California, the counselors in training at Goddard College, the courageous women of Chittenden Regional Correctional Facility located in South Burlington, VT and the addicts of the world—We thank you.

POETS

Jennifer Bradpiece was born and raised in the multifaceted muse, Los Angeles, where she still resides. She often collaborates with multi-media artists on projects. Her poetry has been published in various anthologies, journals, and online zines, including Redactions, Degenerate Literature, and The Common Ground Review. Last year, her manuscript, *Lullabies for End Times*, made the final ten in the Paper Nautilus Debut Serious Chapbook Contest.

Sometimes, 48
In Praise Of Funny Socks, 63
Real, 91

Lynne Bronstein is now a crime writer, with a short story in the anthology Last Resort, and a playwright whose Shakespeare adaptation "As You Like Totally Like It" was produced by the Expressions reading series. She also adds that she's a poet with two Pushcart nominations to her credit.

Free, 11

Casey Brown And Hailey Solis
Casey is too tired to write a bio and Haley wishes he would.

Side Effects, 66

Deanne Meeks Brown is a mother, writer, graduate student, breast cancer survivor, and lead singer in a rock n' roll band. She is currently writing a book for cancer survivors with her professor. You can read about some of her greatest adventures in her blogs: TheYesMom.com and TheYesMomGoesToSchool.com.

Dear Sugar Daddy, 21
Repeat, 42
Transformation, 119

Dan Burkhardt is a resident of Phoenix, AZ. He has been married for 36 years and is the proud father of two daughters and grandfather of one grandson. He has been disabled for over 25 years. His pain has led to many addictive behaviors. His recovery is ongoing.

The Insider, 59

Peggy Carter has found that writing provides her with real perspective on the world's happenings, and her long life provides her with material. She enjoys taking workshops which provide her with new topics. The blank page (or computer screen) doesn't scare her; rather, she is inspired. She has been published in Bellowing Arc, The Stray Branch and Decanto, as well as The Red Fez.

Seduction, 5
This Time, 26
Memory, 90

Marc Cid is a Downey-based poet who enjoys writing, performing, and occasionally submitting poems that tend to leave his audience wondering whether they're supposed to laugh or not. Usually he wants them to, and then to feel bad about it afterwards.

A Happier Ending, 95

Peggy Dobreer (www.peggydobreer.com) has been nominated for one pushcart prize, has one poetry collection, *In the Lake of Your Bones*, and is a longtime educator and movement artist offering a motion-generated poetry experience in her E=Mc2Bodied Poetry Workshops. She was a Program Director for AROHO2015 in Abiquiu, New Mexico and currently teaches Language Arts at Foothill Prep School. One of ten poets to be featured in the first *Aeolian Harp Folio Series* by Glass Lyre Press. Her poetry has been published in *Like a Girl*, *Lucid Moose Lit*, *Cadence Collective Anthology*, *Pirene's Fountain*, *The Bicycle Review*, *WordWright's Magazine*, *LA YogaMagazine*, and most recently in *The Voices of Leimert Park Redux Anthology*, Tsehai Publishers. She has been curating poetry events in Los Angeles for 20 years.

Intervention, 114

Claudia Duran has a BFA from Cargnegie Mellon University and has worked with Casa0101 since 2006. She has written and directed over a dozen shows with and co-founded *Chicanas Cholas y Chisme*. Ms. Duran wrote, directed, and produced feature *Sofia for Now*, which screened at national and international film festivals. Over the years she has received awards for Up And Coming Filmmaker, Best Director, Best Screenplay, and Best Short Film. She has directed webseries and documentaries including *Last Cry for Katrina: Bringing Back The Big Easy*. Theater Credits Include: *After 4 Play*, *A Force to Be Reckoned With*, *Art Share One Acts*, *Chicanas Cholas y Chisme*, *Children of Pelops*, *Drunk Girl*, *Eastside Queer Stories Festival*, *Frida Kahlo Theater 10 Minute Plays*, *Madea*, *Occupy the Heart*, *Short + Sweet Hollywood*, *Sp!t*, *Tango*.

Mi Querida, 34

Becca Gaffron is a sometimes writer, sometimes procrastinator, and hopes she will be forgiven for both. She is fascinated by sea-green spaces, words, and men who behave like cats. Her current works in progress include a fourth novel and an MA in Counseling Psychology from Goddard College.

Jerry Garcia (www.gratefulnotdead.com) is a poet, photographer and filmmaker from Los Angeles, California. He has been a producer and editor of television commercials, documentaries and motion picture previews. His poetry has been seen in various journals and anthologies including, *Wide Awake: Poets of Los Angeles and Beyond, Coiled Serpent Anthology, The Chiron Review, Palabra* and *Askew*. His full-length collection *On Summer Solstice Road* was recently published by Green Tara Press.

John Gardiner lives and writes in Laguna Beach. For many years, he has co-hosted the Laguna Poets Workshop. Gardiner has 12 collections of poems and prose to his credit, including last year's release of *Rogue Waves* by Windflower Press. He teaches part-time at UC Irvine and performs in a rock 'n roll show called "Shakespeare's Fool." Upcoming shows include two performances at the Festival of Arts in Laguna this summer and the New Swan Theatre at UC Irvine.

Austyn Guthrie is your classic 24-year-old California-quintessential who loves love, learning, music and people. He has been writing since second grade, but it wasn't until a Bible Literature class in high school that really got him invested in the beauty of the pen. He primarily writes poetry and songs, and cites his second favorite book, *The Wise Man's Fear*, as a major and bottomless source of inspiration and study.

Donna Hilbert's (www.donnahilbert.com) books include *The Green Season* from World Parade Books, which is a collection of poetry and prose. It is available in an expanded second edition. The work about the death of her husband appears in *Transforming Matter* and in *Traveler in Paradise: New and Selected Poems* from PEARL Editions. Her work is widely anthologized, including *Boomer Girls, A New Geography of Poets, Solace in So Many Words*, most recently in *The Widows' Handbook* from Kent State University Press and *The Doll Collection* from Terrapin Books. Her poems can be found monthly at Verse-Virtual.com.

Trista Hurley-Waxali is an immigrant from Toronto, who finally listened to her parents advice and moved South. She has performed at Avenue 50, Stories Bookstore and internationally at O'bheal in Ireland and for Helsinki Poetry Connection. She writes weird short stories and is working on her novel, *At This Juncture*.

Boris Salvador Ingles was born and raised in Los Angeles, in the small community of Boyle Heights. He combines poetry and photography, as means for visual and emotional expression. A mixture of humor, rawness, vulnerability and a sense for dark street realism. His poems have appeared in *Spectrum, Spectrum 2, Cadence Collective: Year Two Anthology, Then & Now: Conversations With Old Friends* and most recently, *The Coiled Serpent Anthology.*

Elizabeth Isela Szekeresh (www.elizabethisela.com) is a playwright, poet and actor. She writes primarily about mental health, addiction, sexuality and identity. Her ten minute play "A Down and Brown Christmas" was part of the "Fueling Fire: New works by Chingona Writers" at the Chance-a-Ton (Chance Theater 2017). She read her solo show "Paper Plastic Clothes" at the Segundo Jueves Latina/o Play Project (UC Riverside 2015). Elizabeth has performed her solo show "Songleader Gone Bad!" nationally. An excerpt was published in the Latina Studies Journal (2014). Elizabeth is a founding member and the Managing Director of Breath of Fire Latina Theater Ensemble.

Christine Isherwood, BA (Hons) UK, Singer-Songwriter, Dip. Assertiveness Trainer, VMTR, is a Voice Movement Therapist. She works with individual clients, teaches workshops internationally, and supervises VMT students and practitioners. With Anne Brownell, she co-directs and co-teaches the Voice Movement Therapy Training Singing The Psyche/ The Voice Unchained. She has written and performed in political musicals, toured the UK and Europe with theatre groups and bands, and recorded as a pop singer. She has lectured and taught at Liverpool Institute for the

Performing Arts, (LIPA), the Western Australian Academy for Performing Arts (WAAPA), and is adjunct faculty at The Create Institute Expressive Art Therapy program in Toronto, Canada. She lives on Martha's Vineyard and is currently recording an album of death songs.

Cold, hard beds, 32
Rotten, 99
Anaesthia, 117

Betsy Kenoff-Boyd lives in Redondo Beach and has more than enough vices to count on one hand: coffee, kisses, earth porn, book-hoarding and vodka appreciation. She received an MFA from Antioch University in Los Angeles and has been up to no good since then, having spent the last decade teaching ESL to delightful immigrant communities. Currently, she's working on a teaching credential in Special Education through CSU Dominguez Hills. She will be the 3rd generation of LAUSD teachers in her family. Though she appears ageless behind her freckle camouflage she's been writing and publishing poetry since 1986.

After The 2016 Election (And/Or) A Whiskey Shot For Your
Thoughts, My Beloved, 19

Jessica Kirby is a writer, Animal Behaviorist, lecturer, singer, artist, equestrian, and therapeutic riding instructor in Georgia who is currently completing her Master's in Applied Psychology at Goddard College. Her goal is to facilitate a loving, fun, and symbiotic healing relationship between her human and animal clients. She resides with her partner, Fernando, two rescued dogs, Kafka and Rakshasa, and two rescued horses, Chance and Luna, with which she competes in 3 day eventing.

The Hunter Ring, 30

Mike Lemp 75 years old, retired, enjoying computers and writing.

Loving Addiction, 93

Betsy Mars (marsmyst.wordpress.com/) is a writer, educator, mother, and lover of animals, nature, language, and travel - best when all combine. She has spent most of her lifetime dealing with addiction and addictive behavior in one form or another, both in herself, and in her loved ones. Her work has been published by Gnarled Oak, Silver Birch Press, the California Quarterly, and Cadence Collective, as well as in several anthologies.

Perdition, 64
Music From A Farther Room, 80

Ellyn Maybe (ellynmaybe.com) is a Southern California based poet, United States Artist nominee 2012, who has performed both nationally and internationally as a solo artist and with her band. Her work has been included in many anthologies and she is the author of numerous books. She also has a critically acclaimed poetry/music album, *Rodeo for the Sheepish*, from Hen House Studios. In addition to her band, her latest poetry/music project is called ellyn & robbie (ellynandrobbie.com). Their new album is called *Skywriting with Glitter.*
Addiction Subtraction, 94

Terry McCarty began writing poetry in and around--and sometimes about--Southern California in the summer of 1997. From 1998 to 1999, he was a member of the Midnight Special Bookstore poetry workshop in Santa Monica. He has been a featured poet at several venues in California, Nevada, Texas and Washington. Terry's poetry has appeared in two volumes of the "A Poet is a Poet series", plus the Tebot Bach anthology "So Luminous the Wildflowers" and Lummox Press' "The Long Way Home: The Best of the Little Red Book Series."
Fearbasing, 62

Angela Moore is a writer/director/producer/actor with the theater festival Chicanas Cholas y Chisme, and a drummer/singer/song co-writer with the band Daisy Unchained. She also is on the steering committee for the OC Racial Justice Collaborative, working to replace white supremacy with justice for all.
Introducing Life, The Board Game: Addiction Edition!, 121

Ralph Moore (a.skysearch.net) is a father, grandfather, great-grandfather, writer, astrologer and creator of the TRUSA Chart.
Addictions, 60

Raundi Moore-Kondo is a published poet, 2016 Pushcart Nominee, author, teacher, publisher, musician, singer/songwriter and the Founder of *For The Love of Words Creative Writing Collective*. She has been published in several journals and anthologies. She was *L.A. Examiners Pick of the Week, Winner of the Light bulb Mouth Literary Adventure Part V* and was recently published in Spectrum's *Top Ten L.A. Poets of 2017*. When she isn't writing or pushing poetry on people, she is the bassist for the bands *Daisy Unchained* and *Hurt and the Heartbeat*.
A Crooked Sidewalk Followed Me Home, 85
Policy Changes, 106
An Addicts Thriving Guide, 120

Chrissie Morris Brady now lives on the south coast of England, after spending years travelling and living in other countries. She gained her degree in Psychology at the University of Southern California, and is often homesick for L.A. Chrissie has been published by Plum Tree Books, Antiheroin Chic, Dissident Voice, Mad Swirl, Red Leaf Review, Novel Masters, WISHpoetry, Dead Snakes and other poetry publications. Occasionally Chrissie has essays published on subjects to do with human rights. She worked for three years with recovering addicts in the Inland Empire.

Need, 31
Best, 79

Richard Nester has an MFA from the University of Massachusetts and was twice a fellow at the Fine Arts Work Center in Provincetown. His essays on social justice appear frequently in The Catholic Agitator, a publication of the LA Catholic Worker. He was also the featured poet in the 2015 summer issue of Floyd County Moonshine. He has two poetry collections, *Buffalo Laughter* and *Gunpowder Summers*, both published by Kelsay Books.

Hooked, 46

Derrick Ortega's chapbook *Dunes* will be forthcoming from Three Count Pour press and he is fast at work, finishing his first book. He received an MFA in Creative Writing & Writing for the Performing Arts from UC Riverside and a BFA in Creative Writing from Chapman University. His poetry has appeared in Letter [r] Press, Fact-Simile Editions, and elsewhere. He is a creative writing instructor for Orange County School of the Arts in Santa Ana, CA and Poet-in-Residence for Idyllwild Arts Academy in Idyllwild, CA.

Habits (Formerly Known As Jigsaw Limbs), 25
Our Secret Graveyard, 44
Turnaround Trip, 104

Jaimes Palacio: Google Jaimes Palacio! He has written for periodicals, hosted and booked award winning readings like Penguins Hooked on Macaronics and has appeared in numerous anthologies including A Poet is a Poet No Matter How Tall, Attack of the Poems! and a Poet's Haggadah (even though he is not Jewish!). His chapbooks for sale are now all out of print. He is baffled to discover he has become one of the two most requested disc jockeys (his day job) at Fly By Night. Kristen Stewart once liked his poems.

Mother, 71
Insomnia, 98
Why I Share In The Frustration Of The Young Lady And Her
*   Earnest Contemplation Of War, 101*

Cynthia Quevedo is the wife of a man who keeps her laughing, and the mother of three fabulous people. She is honored to have her poems published in *A Poet is a Poet No Matter How Tall; Episode II: Attack of the Poems; Lummox Number Four 2015; Fire in The Treetops, 2015 HNA Anthology;* and *Short Poems Ain't Got Nobody to Love.*
"Scandal", 67

Cindy Rinne (www.fiberverse.com) creates art and writes in San Bernardino, CA. Cindy is the author of several books-in 2017, *Listen to the Codex* from Yak Press, and *Breathe In Daisy, Breathe Out Stones* from FutureCycle Press. She is a founding member of PoetrIE, a literary community and a finalist for the 2016 Hillary Gravendyk Prize. Her poetry appeared or is forthcoming in: *Birds Piled Loosely, CircleShow, Home Planet News, Outlook Springs, The Wild Word (Berlin), Storyscape Journal, Cholla Needles,* and others.
Attachment To Belonging, 13

Linda Singer has been published in a variety of Southern California anthologies and she has featured at several venues in the Los Angeles area. Linda has had two plays produced in Dallas and she sold a script to the TV series, Evening Shade. She is currently involved with the acting troupe, Stop Senior Scams, which performs skits teaching about the scam industry and how it targets seniors.
Addiction, 2

Graham Smith, of Long Beach, is known to be partial to three line poems and pints of Guinness.
Fuck Pumps And Perfume, 4
Tried My Father's Pipe, 45

Clifton Snider is the internationally celebrated author of eleven books of poetry, including *Moonman: New and Selected Poems* and, most recently, *The Beatle Bump*, and four novels: *Loud Whisper, Bare Roots, Wrestling with Angels: A Tale of Two Brothers,* and *The Plymouth Papers.* He pioneered LGBTQ literary studies at Cal State Long Beach. A Jungian/ Queer Literary critic, he has published hundreds of poems, short stories, reviews, and articles internationally, as well as the book, *The Stuff That Dreams Are Made On: A Jungian Interpretation of Literature.* His work has been translated into Arabic, French, Russian, and Spanish.
True Love, 28
The Day Elvis Died, 83

Brittany Thaler's first love is teaching, and her students are her strength in all things. She is the Technical Director and technical theatre educator at

The Studio School, an arts-integration magnet school in Colorado. She is also pursuing a Master's degree in Clinical Mental Health Counseling from Goddard College. Brittany plans to utilize her mental health training with young people, with the goal of teaching them how to navigate the slippery slopes of growing up.

Obsession #2, 7

Murray Thomas (www.gmurraythomas.com) is addicted to writing. He can be found sharing his poetry and other words all over Southern California. He loves his beer too, but not to the point of addiction.

Recycling, 68
The Morning After, 88

Sarah Thursday (www.SarahThursday.com) runs a poetry website called CadenceCollective.net, co-hosts a monthly reading with G. Murray Thomas, and founded Sadie Girl Press as a way to help publish local and emerging poets and artists. Her first full-length poetry collection, *All the Tiny Anchors*, and her CD/chapbook, *How to Unexist*, is available at SadieGirlPress.com.

What To Do With Empty Hands, 3
Your Dark Sunlight, 29
Somatic, 51

Maia Villa (www.maiavilla.com) is a rising actress, writer, and musician. A Los Angeles native, she is most at home between taco trucks and boba tea. In June 2015, she graduated from Bennington College with a BA in Drama and a focus in *Marginalized Identities in Performance*. She has performed in various theatre and sketch comedy productions at Bennington College, Mosaic Lizard Theater (Alhambra, CA), CASA 0101 Theater (Los Angeles, CA), and The Playground Theater (Chicago, IL).

Always Be, 73
Simmer, 76

Harlan Wallner spent nine years in the US Army and was twice deployed to Iraq before leaving the service in 2006. After being honorably discharged he attended the University of Central Florida where he earned a degree in philosophy and psychology. Since 2010 he has been studying and practicing holistic emotional healing, vipassana meditation, holistic nutrition, herbalism, and grief work, in an effort to find ways to heal himself and others. He is currently a Master's candidate at Goddard College, studying Clinical Mental Health Counseling. He lives in Pensacola, Florida.

Altered., 108

Candee Wilde Kondo cherishes the written word. She worked for the Detroit Free Press and United Press International. After a brief stint on Wall Street then in public relations, she returned to her roots in journalism. She hopes to write more fiction.

I Cannot Forget This Number, 116

Josh Jennings Wood is the Director of the Creative Writing Conservatory at the Orange County School of the Arts, an arts magnet in Santa Ana, CA, which serves artistically talented 7th-12th graders. There he teaches a variety of workshops in poetry and prose, advises the national award-winning literary and art magazine, and oversee the program for 160 students. He is a past recipient of the John Fowles Writing Center Award for Fiction and finalist for *Glimmer Train*'s Short Story Award for New Writers, *The North American Review*'s James Hurst Poetry Prize, and the Pablo Neruda Prize for Poetry from *Nimrod*. Josh's poetry also appears in *VOLT, SpiralOrb, DIAGRAM, Berkeley Poetry Review, OccuPoetry*, and elsewhere. Previously, he was managing editor for *dirtcakes*, a journal dedicated to exploring themes suggested by the UN Millennium Development Goals to end extreme poverty. With his wife, he is raising two sons whose combined age is 16.

Heaven & Hell, 61
Prayer For My Mother, 70
Freedom Is Free, 103

Jonathan Yungkans is a Los-Angeles-native poet, writer and photographer with an intense love for the sea and local history. He is currently enrolled in the MFA Writing program at California State University, Long Beach. His works have appeared in *Lime Hawk, Silver Birch Press, Twisted Vine Literary Journal* and other publications.

Coffee, 86
Point Vincente, 97

Chittenden Regional Correctional Facility located in South Burlington, VT is the only women's facility in Vermont. 80% of the women incarcerated at the Chittenden Regional Correctional Facility are mothers to minor children. Lund's Kids A-Part program seeks to reduce the traumatic impact of a mom's incarceration on her children, by providing parenting support to the incarcerated mother, and to support the children's caregivers in the community. Kids-A-Part provides a child-friendly visiting space inside the correctional facility for individual mother-child visits, as well as group visits. Within the program they run a "mom's mail" program to help moms send mail to their children and arrange for weekly phone calls, parenting education, and child development groups for moms.

Kids-a-part also provides financial assistance to caregivers to help facilitate visits for children living outside of Chittenden County, as well as connecting the caregivers to needed resources during the mother's incarceration. The program coordinator and family case manager advocate for family centered thinking within the correctional facility and help make re-entry plans for moms leaving the correctional facility.

The women that submitted these poems are participants in my Family and Future Connections group that takes place on Wednesday evenings, as well as one on one sessions that I offer prior to the group each week. All 3 of these women are serving time for crimes related to their substance use. They are all courageous women that are hoping to maintain recovery once they are released from the facility.

D.B., Resident Of Chittenden Regional Correctional Facility
Heroin Can't Make You A Heroine, 54

N.R., Resident Of Chittenden Regional Correctional Facility
Save Me, 57

T.W., Resident Of Chittenden Regional Correctional Facility
Heroin, 56

Made in the USA
Middletown, DE
25 September 2017